NOT SO
POLITICALLY
CORRECT

NOT SO POLITICALLY CORRECT

A Collection of Laughs, Inspirations, Favorite Emails, and Great Stories

MARTHA HOWALD

NOT SO POLITICALLY CORRECT
A COLLECTION OF LAUGHS, INSPIRATIONS, FAVORITE EMAILS, AND GREAT STORIES

iUniverse books may be ordered through booksellers or by contacting:

iUniverse
1663 Liberty Drive
Bloomington, IN 47403
www.iuniverse.com
1-800-Authors (1-800-288-4677)

When I received these e-mails, they only had the name of the family member or friend on the e-mail. I do not know where these e-mails originated from or who the authors are.

ISBN: 978-1-5320-3027-7 (sc)
ISBN: 978-1-5320-3026-0 (e)

Library of Congress Control Number: 2017914002

Print information available on the last page.

iUniverse rev. date: 01/31/2019

I wish to thank my daughter Amy Welch for her help in last-minute details and preparation for sending my book to the publisher. Also, appreciation of my dear husband with some of the important details of the stories and my many hours at the computer. I was also sincerely blessed with all the help and patience of the publisher (iUniverse). Most of all, I thank the Lord for even giving me the idea that I could possibly write a book.

Contents

My Little Red Boots

WHEN I WAS ABOUT seven years old, I loved doing things with my daddy on the farm. I was what you would call a tomboy. Whenever I was with my dad, I would have to wear my little red boots.

Believe it or not, I always enjoyed helping my dad load manure onto the manure spreader. I had a little pitchfork just like my dad's big pitchfork. I would do my part in scooping up the manure from where the cows, hogs, cattle, or whatever had made the mess and toss it in the manure spreader.

Yes, I did get some up and over into the spreader now and then. It was a little difficult for a seven-year-old little girl to do, but I had fun. I thought I was big stuff and really helping my father. I found out in later years that my dad got quite a kick out of me wanting to be with him and having my help. Ha!

The fun part was riding on the spreader and spreading all that manure over the fields. I'm sure some of it landed on me at times, but it didn't seem to bother me at that age. Now I can't imagine enjoying being around that sort of thing, but times do change with age.

I have great memories of spending that quality time with my daddy.

Lake Erie Vacations

MY FATHER LOVED TO fish, and we would go to Lake Erie on vacations sometimes. He would fish, and the family could spend time on the beach.

We would rent a cabin right on the beach where we could swim and enjoy the water. We would take a huge tractor tire tube that we could blow up, and the whole family would enjoy playing on it together.

At that time, I was very young, maybe eight years old. I remember playing on it with the family. We were laughing and jumping the waves, and all of a sudden, I lost hold and fell away from the tube. Not knowing how to swim and not being able to touch the bottom, I went under. It seemed like an eternity before they finally missed me on the tube. My older brother grabbed me and pulled me up out of the water. I was spitting and sputtering forever, it seemed.

After that happened, I never seemed to enjoy the water. I finally took swimming lessons when I was an adult from a neighbor lady in our subdivision. However, I never really learned to be comfortable in the water. When she required us to dive off the diving board and swim clear to the other end of the pool to pass our swimming tests, I dived in and swam clear to the other end of the pool without coming up for air. I was still scared of not being able to touch the bottom and had never learned the art of treading water.

To this day, I think that experience at Lake Erie affected my love of being in the water. I am much happier with my two feet on the ground.

A few years ago, we went to a water park with our children and grandchildren. They told me that if I went down the slide on a tube, I wouldn't go under the water and I wouldn't get my hair wet. That is another reason I don't like the water. Wrong! I went under, my hair got soaked, my glasses flew off, and I wasn't able to touch the bottom of the pool. I finally made it to the side of the pool, but I was not a very happy camper!

They apologized and said their other grandmother had done it and hadn't gone under. Of course I forgave them and laughed about it.

If I get into a pool, I just stay in the shallow end and stay cool. I prefer everyone to just let me do my thing while they do theirs. That will keep Grammy happy!

Brother in the Service

I WAS IN THE THIRD grade when my brother went into the army to serve his country. I loved my brother very much, and he loved to throw me up in the air and play and tease me. We were very close for being so many years apart. When I was eight years old, he was around twenty years old.

He was stationed in Mississippi, and my folks and I traveled there to see him before he left to go to New Guinea. We were staying in a hotel, and he came and met us in our room. Usually when I saw him, I would run to him and jump into his arms. For some unknown reason, that time I wanted nothing to do with him. My parents were so disappointed in me. The only thing anyone could come up with was that his army uniform made me very afraid of him.

I guess I was just young enough that I wasn't familiar with the uniform, hat, and haircut. It really caused me to be afraid. It also had been some time since I had seen him. I still remember this because it was a very emotional time for me, and our emotions have a lot to do with our memories.

My parents were pretty upset because they had taken me so he could see me. I knew I was doing something wrong, but I couldn't help myself. We don't understand how change can really affect the feelings of a child. Hearing the news and talk at that time about the war could have been part of it also.

I remember Mom sending him boxes of goodies. She would make homemade caramels, and the other kids did not get one piece. It all went to my brother. She would also make him angel food cake and pack it in popcorn. All the boxes looked so good, and I almost wished I were in the army.

My brother was a radioman in New Guinea, and it was a very tough time for him. He lost many of his buddies during the war. It took him some time when he returned home to become like his old self. We really don't appreciate our servicemen and servicewomen like we should or show them that we do.

Favorite Fourth Grade Teacher

WHEN I WAS IN the fourth grade, Miss Hill was my favorite teacher. She was very pretty too. I remember little things like how she would hold her book when she was reading a story to us. I would try to hold my book the same way. I tried doing many things just like she did them.

When my older brother arrived home from serving in the army, he met Miss Hill in her father's grocery store. The next thing I found out was that he was dating my favorite teacher. I was so excited and proud. I was telling all my classmates at school that my brother was dating Miss Hill. He would show up at school now and then to see her, and I would be so proud and feel so special.

It wasn't too long before they got married, and by that time, I had moved on to the sixth grade. My sixth grade teacher was the sister of my new sister-in-law. I again made sure that all my classmates knew this. She was very nice and was my second-favorite teacher in grade school.

Odd Development

DID YOU EVER HEAR of someone buying a new house and not noticing that a very important item was missing until after he or she had moved in?

Since this was an older couple, we will give them an excuse for not noticing.

While moving in, Louise needed to use the bathroom. She looked all around and realized that what she needed right then was missing. She shouted for her husband. He came running as fast as he could at his age, and she said, "Jim, you are not going to believe this. Do you see something missing that I need right now?" She quickly made arrangements for her situation.

After talking the problem over, they agreed they needed to write a letter to the man who had sold them this house. Jim was so upset that he insisted his wife write the letter. She thought and thought about how to explain the missing problem to the seller. People didn't use the word *toilet* back then. After putting some more thought to it, the word *bathroom commode* came to her mind. That would work perfectly. She could use the initials BC, and he would understand what she was talking about.

The seller received the letter, and knowing these people were Christians, he knew that BC meant *Baptist church*.

Dear Mrs. Holder:

To answer your question to the missing problem, the BC is only five miles down the road from your home. It is quite large, seating around 185 people. If you go regularly, you need to know a large number of people like to take their lunch and make a day of it, visiting with other people while seated there. This really pains me not to go more regularly, especially in the very cold weather. I hope this answers your question about the missing item. I also hope to see you there and see more of you at that time.

Yours truly,

The Seller

Memories of Grandparents

A GOOD MEMORY WHEN I was eleven years old was having the blessing of my grandparents living just across the road from us. We were farmers and lived in the country.

I loved my grandparents, as most grandchildren do, and I spent as much time with them as I was allowed. My parents didn't want me to make a nuisance of myself.

Being farmers, my father worked in the fields until it got dark. We didn't have supper until around seven. My grandparents always ate early, around five. When I could, I would walk over to their house at their suppertime. It was fun to watch them eat and see what they were having. They had their main meal at lunchtime and leftovers or "make do" for supper.

Many times, my grandpa would be eating a bowl of bread and milk with salt and pepper sprinkled over it. He would also eat a big onion. He would either cut large slices or just take a big bite out of the onion like an apple. Yuck. It looked pretty gross to me, but he sure seemed to enjoy it. As I got older, I found out that a big bowl of toasted bread, sugar, and milk made a great after-school snack.

I also noticed how he used his knife a lot, especially if he was eating peas. He would scoop them up with his knife instead of using his spoon as most people do. I was fascinated by how he could keep those peas on his knife without them rolling off.

My grandma would make delicious, thick maple syrup to put on our biscuits. I could take a big spoonful of it, and it wouldn't run all over the place. While I was visiting with them and watching them eat, she would always fix me a biscuit with some of that delicious syrup on it. She wouldn't feed me too much because she didn't want to spoil my supper, knowing that we would be eating later.

Another memory I enjoyed when visiting them was they would have a card table set up with a jigsaw puzzle in the making. I enjoyed sitting there while Grandpa found pieces to fit. He always bragged on me when I did, which we sometimes forget to do as parents and grandparents. Little things are so important to children.

Grandpa always had a special candy dish in a special place that he offered us kids. It was always full of the kind we especially liked. It was just a little thing that was special for us.

I have found the importance of showing your children and grandchildren love in small ways. It doesn't always have to be a big special event. We remember the small things.

Easter Sunrise Morning

WHEN WE WERE KIDS, we always enjoyed getting up early and getting dressed up in our new Easter clothes, and going to the Easter sunrise service. Our parents didn't go because they had to do the chores that needed to be done on the farm: milking the cows, feeding the chickens, and caring for all the other animals. They would, however, always go to church later with my brother and me. My older brother and sisters were married and had their own homes.

When we would come home from the sunrise service, we always had a few hours to kill before it was time to go to church.

My brother and I both played the piano, and that morning, we decided at the same moment to play the piano. We both headed for it, knowing what was in our minds.

He slid in on one end, and I sat on the other end of the piano bench. He shoved me, and I shoved him. We ended up in a real battle about who was going to win out in the end. It went from shoving each other to actually pushing and hitting.

We were still dressed in our new clothes. I was wearing silk hose, a hat, and a veil. My hair and makeup were done. Well, my hose ended up with runs, my veil was torn, and my hat was cockeyed. My face was red, and my makeup was running from the tears that were falling. Oh, yes, he came out unharmed!

Right at the end of this big powwow, my sister and her husband walked in. They could definitely tell that whatever had gone on was not a good thing.

Mom came in from the barn and could also tell that we had been up to no good. We were both old enough to know better, but we were both only thinking of ourselves and what we wanted to do. We got a talking to and asked forgiveness of each other. I had to do a complete makeover before I could go to church.

I couldn't believe that happened after we had just been at the sunrise service. I guess it didn't do us much good that morning. We had to ask God's forgiveness also. Neither of us got to play the piano—so all that was for nothing. I think that was the last scuffle we ever had, and we have laughed about it many times since. I guess it is normal for siblings to do crazy things like that every once in a while.

We have always had much love for one another in our family, and it has grown over the years.

Best to Obey Parents

MY PARENTS LIVED IN Ohio on a farm and spent a lot of their time visiting Florida. They had a small trailer they lived in while there.

My brother and I visited at Christmas and loved to go to Cocoa Beach. Many people would drive their cars on the beach, but Father specifically told us not to drive on the beach. When we arrived there, we noticed other people were driving and parking on the beach—so why not us?

We were having such a great time swimming and sunbathing that we completely forgot about the time. We saw other people leaving, but we didn't think about why. We finally noticed the tide was beginning to come in, and then we knew why people were leaving. We decided to get out of there fast. When we got to the car, we were stuck in the sand. We had parked in the soft sand instead of where it was more solid.

All of a sudden, we noticed that we were the only car left on the beach. My brother was trying to get us out, but the tires were sinking deeper and deeper. The next thing we knew, we were down to the axle. We were both getting scared, wondering what our dad was going to do if we didn't get the car out before the water came up. We should have listened, and now we know why he told us not to drive on the beach. As usual, parents know best.

I guess it was a rule that a security truck checked to see if anyone was still on the beach when the tide came in. We were so happy to see him. He pulled us out, and we headed home, thinking about what we were going to tell Dad. We knew he would see the sand on the axle, so we had to be honest and tell him we disobeyed.

He explained why it is best to obey. There is almost always a reason why parents tell you not to do something. It's not because they enjoy telling you no. It is for your own good. We never drove on the beach after that—even though many other cars were doing it. I think God had a hand in that. He was teaching us it is always best to obey your parents and God!

Bragging Can Backfire

I ALWAYS LOVED TO BAKE, and pies were one of my favorite desserts to eat. I almost always had a homemade pie on hand.

When I would bake pies, I would usually bake twelve pies at a time and freeze them. Some farmers close by would come over when the weather was bad or use some excuse to come over and play pinochle with my husband and me. Of course, they always expected one of those pies to come out of the freezer and find its way to the oven so they could enjoy Martha's pie.

I was known for my pie baking. I was told that my piecrusts were extra flaky, and that was one reason the pies were so good. During a Christmas break, my brother and I visited my parents in Florida. While there, they wanted me to make one of my famous pies.

I got busy and made a pie shell for an open-crust pie. When I took it out of the oven, it looked beautiful. It was a lovely shade of light brown. I thought I would break off a little piece to see how tender and flaky it was. I tried and said, "Oh my goodness." I couldn't break off a piece. I couldn't figure out what had happened. I picked it up, took it outside, and tried breaking it in two.

My brother joined me in my attempt to break it. Of course, he was dying laughing at my famous piecrust. We threw it up against a tree, but the doggone thing just wouldn't break. I went back into the house to check the ingredients I had used to put it together. I quickly realized I had baked a piece of pottery because I had forgotten the oil. Yes, I had to eat humble pie that day.

PRize Cake

WHEN I WAS IN high school, my mother taught me how to make angel food cake. They were not the easiest cakes to make. This cake took thirteen eggs, and I had to do everything just right when blending them with the other ingredients in order to end up with a cake that was light, tender, and had risen very high.

We had what we called a fall festival or a community conference every year in our small town. It was a little like a small fair. People would bring things they had made over the year—homemade sewing projects, quilts, canned goods, fruits and vegetables, plants, baked goods, and many other things.

One lady in the community always won the grand champion prize cake, which was an angel food cake. Mother suggested that I enter the contest as a junior in high school. The lady who usually won happened to be the aunt of the boy I had been dating. I resisted for some time, but I finally gave in and decided to give it a try. None of the things entered had names on them, so the judges never knew who made the items.

When the judging took place, I was in school. I couldn't wait to see what would happen. When I entered the gym where all the items were, the big blue grand champion ribbon was beside my cake. I was overjoyed that I had won, but I knew my boyfriend's aunt would not be too happy about it.

When it came time for the next year's conference, my parents were in Florida. My girlfriends at school said, "Your mom isn't here this year to help you bake the cake. You probably won't win."

When the time came to bake the cake, I was nervous and fearful. *What if I don't win this year? They will think my mom helped me bake it—and she didn't.* I finally decided not to worry about it and just proceeded like I always did. When I took it out of the oven, it looked like it had risen even higher than normal. When I finished swirling the fluffy pink frosting on it, it looked beautiful. The aunt's cake looked great also.

When the judging was over, I couldn't believe what had happened. The big blue grand champion ribbon was beside my cake again. The aunt's cake had the grand-prize ribbon. My friends quickly said, "I guess you do bake those cakes."

I always asked and appreciated the Lord's help, and I know I had it. I am sad because I misplaced the recipe for my angel food cake. I guess that was for a season—as many other things are also for a season in our lives.

Miracles Do Happen

WHEN SOME WOMEN HAVE problems during pregnancy, they are required to remain in bed for the rest of the pregnancy. This happened to Stacey, but it did not prevent Susie from being born very prematurely. She weighed no more than two pounds eight ounces and was only eight and a half inches long.

The doctor said, "Not sure she will live through the night. If she does, she could be totally retarded and not be able to live a normal life." Stacey would absolutely not accept that kind of news.

That night, little Susie held on. As the time passed, Stacey became even more determined that Susie would make it. Jim, her father, was not so sure because he had overheard the doctors talking. What he heard was not good news for little Susie. Jim thought they should consider making some arrangements in case they lost her. Stacey would not give in to any negative talk about Susie.

She had many wires attached to her body, and Susie hung on hour after hour. This encouraged them, but the doctor brought them very discouraging news. He presented them with a new problem. Her nerve system would not allow them to hold her. They could barely touch her. In the midst of all the wires and tubes, they could only pray God would hold her close to Him.

As time moved on, Susie slowly gained an ounce or two. The nerve problem got better, allowing the parents to finally hold her in their arms. She continued to become stronger as the days went on, and she turned four months old. The doctors continued to warn them that she still might not survive, but he allowed them to take her home from the hospital.

Five years passed, and Susie was beautiful and full of energy and life. She was very small and petite, but she was everything a little girl can be and more.

One hot afternoon in 2005 in Oklahoma, Susie and her mother were watching her brother play tennis at his school. Susie got very quiet and said, "Do you smell that?"

"Yes," her mother said. "It smells like rain."

"No, don't you smell Him? It smells like Him when he held me on His chest." She then ran off to play.

This confirmed that, even though they could not hold Susie in their arms, God was holding her on His chest. Susie remembered His sweet loving scent. God knew what Susie needed at that time and takes our place when necessary. God heard the families' many prayers and took their place.

What a God we have!

My Predicament!

In 1951, I was a junior in high school. At the time, I was dating a boy who was a senior. A school that was located about twelve miles from us consolidated with our school. A new boy from that school happened to be in my class.

I was a cheerleader for our basketball team, and at one of our games, my sister was sitting in the bleachers. When she got my attention, she motioned for me to come up to the bleachers. When I got up there, she asked, "Who was that boy you were just talking to?"

I said, "Oh, he is a new boy who just came to our school."

She said, "Wow. He is really a good-looking guy. You should date him."

As I got to know him, I thought he was pretty good-looking and super nice. He had dark, wavy hair.

The next thing I knew, he appeared at my house to ask for a date. I thought, *Gee, he must really want to date me because everyone knows I am dating another boy.* He sat down in our family room and talked with my father for quite a while. I finally asked him if he wanted to go to our living room so we could talk. My father really liked him because not many boys want to talk to a girl's father. Usually they are shy or fearful of any contact with them.

I finally accepted his offer for a date on Thanksgiving. We went on a double date with his sister and her fiancé. We went to see *The African Queen*. To this day, it is still one of my favorite movies.

In December, my boyfriend was attending college. He had a habit of calling at the last minute when he got home for the weekend. The phone rang, and he said, "I'm home, and I will be right there." Lo and behold, I had already accepted a date with the new good-looking guy. I stood there with the phone in my hand, lost for words. I finally put the phone back on the hook and went looking for help from my family.

My brother was also home from college, and I asked him for advice.

He started laughing, getting a big kick out of my situation. No pity at all. His comment was exactly what a brother's would be. He said, "Hey, you got yourself into this—you can get yourself out." My mother more or less repeated my brother's response. They both were laughing at my predicament.

I asked if they could answer the door and make some excuse for me, but they wouldn't. One thing that made it even more difficult was that I was leaving the next morning to go to Florida with my parents.

I finally decided to go out with the first one who got to my house. Well, my college boyfriend arrived first. My other friend lived on a big dairy farm and always had chores to do. The cows had to be milked at the same time every morning and night, which usually made him late. It was hard to compete with the cows when their needs were bigger than mine.

He finally showed up after my boyfriend and I had left. My brother went to the door. My friend asked if I was there, and my brother told him I wasn't home. My new friend said that he would come back later.

When he came back, my brother told him the same thing. My new friend decided to go over to the garage to see if the car was there. If the car was there, then he assumed that I was with someone—probably the old boyfriend. Sure enough, the car was there. The poor guy went back to the house and knocked again. This time, he gave my brother a Christmas gift to give me.

When I arrived home, I felt so bad for all he had gone through—and he had even left me a gift. I wouldn't have an opportunity to explain what happened. When I got to Florida, the first thing I did was write him a note to apologize and explain the whole story.

I quickly received a letter back from him. I had been chosen homecoming queen. He was a very forgiving guy, and from then on, I never dated anyone else. We graduated in 1952, and in 1953, we became husband and wife. We have been married for sixty-three years and have never been sorry. He is still a super nice and forgiving guy, and he is definitely the man God chose for me. I always say, "God had to go to a lot of work to consolidate two schools for us to find each other, but as the Bible says, nothing is too difficult for the Lord."

Missing Tooth

DURING MY SENIOR YEAR of high school, I was dating a boy who is now my husband. He was on the baseball team, and they were practicing out on the field during lunch.

I happened to walk by, and according to him, he took his eyes off the ball. It hit him in the mouth and knocked out one of his front teeth. When they came in from practice, I was standing at the water fountain. He came up to me, held out his tooth, and dropped it in my hand. When I looked at him, I could see he was missing a tooth. I wasn't quite sure what I was supposed to do with that tooth, but I kept it for the time being.

His excuse for missing the catch was that he took his eyes off the ball and was watching me. I don't know if he was telling the truth about that, but it sounded better than just missing the ball.

The dentist wanted to replace it with a gold tooth. Frank immediately rejected that choice, but the doctor said it was the only thing he would do. They quickly went to another dentist, and he replaced it with a bridge to match his other teeth.

I always thought he was a great-looking guy, and the bridge didn't take anything away from him. Due to a later accident, he had to have another partial plate put in. He still is the best-looking guy I know. When he takes out his removable plate, I have to kid him about making the wrong choice for a husband.

Could You Have Met This Challenge?

A FRIEND WAS TELLING ME she had read about students who were very hard to handle. Teachers would come and go, and none of them were able to handle them. Finally, just out of college, Jonathan showed up at the principal's office to apply for this job.

The principal, thinking of the older teachers—with probably more wisdom than this young kid—who couldn't handle these rowdy kids, how in the world could this young kid handle them? The principal said, "Are you sure you want to start your very first job with a challenge like this? I don't want to discourage you, but this could be very tough."

Jonathan was a Christian. He quickly sent a prayer up to the Lord and said, "Sir, please, just give me an opportunity to try."

Jonathan had been preparing himself with lots of prayer prior to the first day of school. He was asking God to give him wisdom in how to approach these kids. The first day finally came, and Jonathan asked God for all the help He could give. As he stood before the class, he said, "Students, I came here today with great excitement. I am very eager to meet you all and get to know each of you personally and hopefully become good friends. When I was your age, I had some really good relationships with my teachers, and I want to be the same for each of you. I hope you all will give me that opportunity. I also came here today to conduct school, but I must have your help."

The biggest guy in the room, Joe, whispered to his buddies, "I can take care of this young squirt and have some fun doing it."

Jonathan told them that there would have to be some rules. "I know none of us really likes to have rules, but I'm going to allow you to make the rules. I will list them on the blackboard as you call them out."

Wow. This is certainly different, the students thought. *This might be interesting.*

Almost instantly, they started shouting out rules. "No fighting." "Don't be late to class." "Show respect to each other." "No stealing allowed."

Jonathan then said, "Next, we have to decide what the punishment should be for breaking these rules. Rules are no good unless they are enforced."

Someone said, "They should receive eight strikes with a rod across their back, and they could not wear a coat for any padding."

No coat? Wow, Jonathan thought. *This is pretty harsh punishment.* "Do you all agree on this punishment?"

Surprisingly, the class agreed.

Jonathan was praising the Lord for his help because everything seemed to be going really well.

A couple of weeks went by, and Joe said, "Someone stole my lunch."

They soon found out it was little Tommy. The teacher talked to Tommy, and he admitted he had taken Big Joe's lunch.

"Tommy, do you remember the punishment for this?"

Little Tommy nodded and said, "Please, don't make me take my coat off." He was wearing a huge coat.

"Remember the rules, Tommy? The coat has to come off."

Tommy didn't even have a shirt on, and he was nothing but skin and bones.

"Tommy, why did you come to school without a shirt on?" Jonathan asked.

Tommy replied, "We are very poor, and my daddy died. Mama can only afford for me to have one shirt, and she is washing it today. This is my big brother's coat, and he let me wear it today to keep warm."

How could he touch this child with a rod—let alone eight times? He knew he must obey the rules or the children would not obey the rules. As he drew back to strike Tommy, Joe hollered out, "Wait. What if I took his whipping for him? Is that allowed?"

"Can't think of a reason you couldn't. Are you sure you want to do this?" Jonathan asked.

Big Joe quickly threw off his coat and stooped over little Tommy at the desk. Slowly, the teacher began to lay the rod on that big back. After only three strikes, the old rod broke in half.

Jonathan began to sob, and then he heard others crying. He looked up to see that everyone in the room had tears streaming down their faces. Tommy had grabbed Joe's neck and was telling him how sorry he was for stealing his lunch. "I knew that was against the rules, but your lunch looked so good. Please forgive me. Big Joe, I will love you till the day I die for taking that whipping for me!"

Big Joe said, "Little Tommy, you are forgiven."

Wow. When we think about it, this is exactly like the beating Jesus took for our sins. He shed His blood on the cross so that you and I could have eternal life with Him in heaven. We are unworthy of the price He paid for us, but aren't you glad He loves us that much?

Farming Can Be Dangerous

When my husband was still in school, his father asked him to plow a field for a disabled neighbor. Because he was still in school, he had to plow at night, using the lights on the tractor.

He loved to sing, even while driving the tractor. The neighbors could often hear him singing from their homes. While plowing and singing, something told him to stop in the middle of the field. He didn't really understand, but he stopped the tractor.

When he looked around, the plow was just over his head. In a few more seconds, it would have come down on his head—and it probably would have killed him. The top part of the hitch had broken, which had allowed the plow to pivot and go up. It was on its way down.

He gives all the credit to the Lord for saving his life. There are many times that the Lord nudges us in different ways, and we ignore Him. It pays to keep tuned in to the Lord.

My First Flight Overseas

MY HUSBAND WAS IN the army and spent two years in Germany in 1956 and 1957.

In February 1956, I was able to fly over and be with him. I flew from Columbus, Ohio, to New York. My sister took me to the airport and gave me strict instructions to call before I got on the plane for Paris, which was my first destination.

I had never flown before, and it was a big, scary experience for me. I wanted to be with my husband and was willing to do anything to be with him. I arrived in New York safely, and everything was going well. When it was nearing the time to board the plane for Paris, I checked the schedule and decided to call my sister.

After calling her, I went back to wait until they called us to board the plane. The schedule had changed. It was now leaving in two hours. I decided against calling my sister again, thinking everything would be fine. The next time I checked the schedule, it was four hours. Later, it was five hours. A weird guy kept eyeing me, which was a bit scary. I kept moving to different areas—but not too far in case there was another change. I was twenty-one and hadn't traveled by myself, especially on a plane traveling overseas.

Finally, after twelve hours, we were able to board. I was exhausted from the stress and fear. I was so happy to finally be on my way to Paris. However, I knew that I had missed some of my future flights. What would I do?

When I arrived in Paris, a lady came on the plane and informed me that I had missed my connecting flight. She said I could either take a train to Frankfurt, Germany, or they would put me up in a hotel. I had been fortunate enough to meet another girl who was also going to Kaiserslautern. She had already had to stay overnight and wanted to get on her way. I decided to go with her on the train.

We decided to split the cost of calling our husbands to let them know we would be coming to the train station rather than the airport. We paged our husbands at the airport, but her husband wasn't there. She assumed he had gone back to the base because she was a day late. He would have needed to get back to the base. I called Frank, and he kept asking why I had missed the plane. He thought it was my fault and seemed a little upset. I told him to listen. We had a really bad connection, and he couldn't hear what I was saying about meeting him at the train station instead of the airport. Because there was so much static, I tried making train sounds and different things to make him understand where to meet me.

When we finally arrived in Frankfurt, I could not find Frank. Thankfully, some American soldiers asked me where I was going. I told them my situation and said I wanted to go to the airport—where I assumed he was waiting—as fast as I could go.

They grabbed me by my arms, picked up my luggage, and took me where I could change my money into marks. They put me in a taxi, and I headed to the airport. No husband again. He had been at the train station, but he didn't see me. He got on the shuttle and went back to the airport. If I had taken the shuttle, we would have met on it.

We grabbed something to eat and then went to a hotel. I was exhausted. I got into the bed, and it felt like things were biting or crawling all over me. We got up, checked the bed, and found nothing. I got back in bed, and the same thing happened. We even removed the sheets, but we still didn't see anything. Finally, Frank decided we were getting out of there. We took the train back to Kaiserslautern. We decided it was probably a combination of nerves, complete exhaustion, and no sleep. It was just too much. It was a very nice hotel—so I don't think we could blame my problem on that.

After arriving at our apartment, I was fine. It was one room upstairs in a German family's home. We slept on a little pullout couch and used their kitchen. We had to share the bathroom with the family and could only have a real bath once a week to help them with the expense of water. They were a lovely family, and we enjoyed our time with them.

During our time in Kaiserslautern, we had met a great couple from Oklahoma and did many things with them. The guys would save up their money, and when they had some time off, we would take some trips. When his time was up, they returned to the United States.

We met another great couple from Atlanta. They were living in a small town called Otterberg. They talked us into moving there. They had an old Opal car for our transportation, and we were only a few miles from Kaiserslautern.

We found a German family that rented rooms to American soldiers. They were wonderful people with two children.

We had the living room, and they spent their evenings around the kitchen table. We shared the kitchen and the bathroom. We had a bedroom with a twin bed and big comforter that was so thick it would stand straight out over us, letting all the cold air come in on the sides. We got used to sleeping in a twin bed, and we didn't have any trouble keeping warm. In the wintertime, it would get really cold.

We mentioned to the Herr that we were going to go buy a Christmas tree.

"Ah nein, nein. I get you Christmas tree in the woods."

Earl came with his black Opal, and headed for the woods. The Herr used an ax to cut down the tree.

It was against the law in Germany to cut down trees. The Herr gave Earl strict instructions about where to let them out. Earl was to drive on and come back in twenty minutes to pick them up.

The Herr and Frank ran into the woods, watching at all times to make sure no one was around to see them. Frank kept pointing to different trees, but they didn't satisfy the Herr. Finally, the Herr found one he liked and cut the top off a good-sized tree. They carried the tree toward the road, hiding behind trees as they went and making sure no one was around to see them with the tree. They watched for Earl and jumped into the car, putting the tree in the back. Earl made a quick getaway. They felt like they were members of the Mafia—black Opal and all. They got the tree home safely, and we really appreciated the Herr going to all that trouble for us. However, they were able to enjoy the decorated tree also.

They didn't have a refrigerator. We had purchased a steak at the commissary and put it outside our bedroom window. The next morning, it had disappeared. The Herr was so distressed that he went out and bought an apartment-sized refrigerator, which was a great expense for him. We again really appreciated his thoughtfulness and concern for us.

Another great memory was their two-year-old boy. Volgar had long, beautiful curly blond hair. It was a family tradition to get their first haircut when they turned two years old. I felt very honored when they asked me to give him his first haircut. It was quite an important occasion to cut off those beautiful curls. I gave them several curls to keep so they could show him the curly hair he had when he was young.

Our friends had an opportunity to adopt a French baby. She was only a few weeks old. Nancy was working and couldn't quit her job right away. They asked me to keep her during the daytime until Nancy could get free from her job in a few weeks.

When they brought Renae home from the agency, she had terrible cradle cap. Even her little face was all red and broken out. The agency told them to keep using lots of oil to get rid of it. I thought the oil was making her worse, and I used good old Ivory soap for her baths. I purchased a fine-toothed comb and worked on the cradle cap. Within a week, it was completely cleared up. Her face was clean and as smooth as silk.

She was a beautiful child. They had been married for several years and were not able to have children. She was such a joy to them. I enjoyed every minute with her and considered it a privilege to care for her.

We left Germany on an old World War II troop ship. Frank was in the lower bow area, and I was in a room with three other girls on deck level. I was told to eat all the time because it would help me avoid getting seasick. That didn't sound right to me, but I thought it would be worth a try. That's exactly what I did, and I didn't get sick. In between meals, I would eat crackers, candy bars, and whatever else was available. The other girls wouldn't eat, and they all got terrible seasickness.

We were in a terrible storm one night. The bow of the boat would come way up out of the water and then go down with a terrible crash. The stern would come up out of the water, and the propellers would spin, shaking the ship like it was going to fall apart. We held our breath every time it would rise and then come down. For hours, I was wondering how Frank was doing down in the lower bow. We finally ran out of the storm, and things calmed down. It happened at night, but there was no sleeping going on. We were hoping we were going to make it. Those ships must have been strong to take that beating.

After eleven days, we passed the Statue of Liberty. What a joy to pull in and dock in New York—the good old United States. The first thing we headed for was McDonald's. We couldn't wait to munch on a hamburger. Can you believe it?

Living in Europe

WHILE MY HUSBAND WAS in Germany, we saved some money and traveled whenever he would get time off or a furlough. A soldier made a very small amount of money back then. We would go on bus tours since we didn't have any other way to travel. Some of our friends would go with us.

We went to Italy and were told not to drink the water there. We were not big drinkers, but we would carry little bottles of Chianti in cute little baskets wherever we went. We had to get used to it since we didn't have bottled water back then.

In Italy, we stopped one night for dinner at a nice restaurant. Our tour guide told us that he would order the wine for us. They brought the wine, and after a few sips, my friend and I got silly and talkative. We realized later why our tour guide wanted to order the wine. Apparently, he ordered something pretty powerful.

We had to check the bathrooms shortly after arriving there and sipping the wine. The restroom was the strangest thing we had ever seen. There were two very large footsteps on each side of a large porcelain hole. We started cracking up. We thought we were in the men's room. We quickly dashed out and went into the other room, thinking it must be the women's room. Oh, no—it was the same as the other one. We were laughing our heads off and having trouble walking. We went to get the guys because we wanted them to see it. Of course, it wasn't near as funny to them.

I guess the wine hadn't affected them like it did us. We decided we didn't need to use the restroom at that place.

By the time we finished dinner, we all felt a little high. After that night, we told the tour guide we would order our own wine.

We also went to the Isle of Capri. The water was absolutely beautiful, but the beach was nothing but small rocks. It was very hard to walk on.

I would wade into the water and then go back and sit on the rocks. We had no sunscreen, and I ended up with a terrible burn on my ankles and feet. They got so red and swollen that I couldn't even get my shoes on.

The people on the bus had all kinds of suggestions for them. One person said I should soak them in hot water, and another person told me to soak them in ice water. Neither idea sounded very good.

The bus stopped at a pharmacy, and my husband tried to explain to the pharmacist what he needed. He couldn't make him understand. Frank and our friend made a seat with their arms and carried me into the store.

When the pharmacist saw me, he immediately knew that I needed a tube of Nivea cream. The cream helped, but it took a while. He told me it would help if I kept my feet elevated. I sat on the bus with my feet in my husband's lap. I'm sure it wasn't very comfortable for him, but he never complained.

We had a great time on all our trips in Europe and made many memories.

Wow!

THIS STORY WILL MAKE you think about how important our lives are to God—and how important God is to us.

In college, Benjamin was in the habit of going to the pool late at night. He was in his twenties and was training to be a diver. Benjamin was never much for attending church, and his family never took him to church. He did, however, have a close friend who often talked to him about what Jesus meant to him. Benjamin never really gave much thought to what Justin was telling him about God. He had more important things he was involved in. As a young man, he was only interested in what his future had in store for him—not what God had planned for his future. He really didn't have time for God.

When he entered the pool area, there were no lights on, which was unusual. He decided the skylight gave him enough light to make his way to the pool and make a few practice dives. As he climbed up the highest diving board, he turned with his back to the pool. As he was perching on the edge of the board with his toes, he stretched his arms out before the jump. He stopped, and his eyes were drawn to a vision on the back wall. It was his shadow in the shape of a cross. It had never happened before.

He stared at the vision. A very strange feeling came over him. He had never felt it before. It was like someone was talking to him. God has a way of getting our attention, and we just have to be willing to listen. Instead of diving, he had the desire to kneel down and ask God to come into his life. All we have to do is ask—and God responds immediately.

The young man stood and was planning to proceed with his dive. At that very important moment, the door opened. A janitor walked in and turned on the lights. As Benjamin looked down at the pool, he realized God had protected him. There was no water in the pool. It had been drained for repairs. Again, God cares and performs His miracles just when we need them.

The Joy of Leading the Choir

WE HAD THE PLEASURE of being involved with music in churches we were attending. It started in a little Baptist church in Radnor, Ohio, in 1954. We were members of the choir, and Frank sang a lot of solos. We also sang duets.

We moved to Florida in 1963 and became involved in starting a branch church sponsored by the First Baptist church in Cocoa, Florida. My husband became the music director, and I was the pianist at the Rockledge Baptist Church.

As time moved on, we had a nice-sized choir. We would practice hard and present cantatas at Christmas and sometimes Easter. It was a very special time in our lives to have that opportunity, and the choir was quite good.

On Sundays, the choir sometimes looked out at the congregation and noticed some of the deacons sleeping on the back row. They would whisper to each other and point at the sleeping deacons. At the end of one particular service, Frank asked everyone to stand. He picked "Open Mine Eyes That I Might See." The choir was cracking up at his choice of hymn. It was so appropriate!

I sang in a trio, and Frank sang in a quartet. I also played piano for the men's quartet. The Ramblers traveled around and sang at different churches in the area. We had quartet practice every Monday night for several years.

We were singing at one church where the stage had small, narrow steps. Our tenor missed the step, and as he threw himself back to catch himself, a button popped off his coat. The button landed right in his hand, which created quite a bit of laughter from the congregation. On the way home, we all laughed hysterically. We had many fun and laughable moments and wonderful memories on those Monday nights.

During that time, I became pregnant. After our daughter was born and was old enough to reach the piano keys, we noticed how she would hit a key on the piano and keep a perfect beat with the music. As she grew up, she always had perfect timing and perfect pitch. She was always good at music, and for a time, she even played and sang in a band. We always gave credit to those nights of practice while I was carrying her during my pregnancy.

The girl who took my place playing the piano in church while I was recuperating got pregnant right away. When I took it over again, I got pregnant again right away. We finally decided it had something to do with that doggone piano bench. Ha!

As the years went by, we moved to a different church as music director and pianist. Again, we had many memorable times during those years of ministering in music.

Coming through the Rye

AT ONE POINT, WE lived in a big brick house on my father's farming land. At times, they would ask for my help in driving the tractor for a certain job. They were combining wheat and asked me to help drive the tractor and wagon so they could empty the wheat bin from the combine into the wagon.

The directions I received from my husband were the following: I was to watch from our porch, and if my husband waved his hat, I was to come across the field with the wagon. If he just waved his hand, I was to come around the field.

I was watching closely and with great anticipation. I saw him wave his hat and got on the tractor. I went through the gate of the wheat field and straight toward them with the wagon. I noticed they were watching me as I came. My dad threw down his hat and started waving to me. I didn't understand, but it looked like they were a bit upset. I started weaving back and forth with the wagon. Finally, they both started waving to me to just come straight. I thought I might be doing something wrong, but I was following my husband's directions. I found out that across the field meant around the inside of the fence—and around the field meant outside the field along the fence. By the time I got to them, they were laughing. They forgave me for smashing some of the wheat when I was traveling across the field.

I never lived that down. The story traveled all over our little country community, and whenever I would meet up with farmers in the area, they would start singing "Coming through the Rye."

I don't remember them asking me to drive the tractor or asking for my help again. I don't know why.

Redneck Letter

My dearest redneck son, Jimmie,

I know you can't read fast, so I'm trying to write this really slow, Jimmie. It's important that I write to tell you we don't live where we did. A friend of your dad's told him he read that most accidents happen within ten miles of your home, so we moved. I wanted to send you the address, but the last people took the house numbers when they left so they wouldn't have to change their address.

This place is really special, and you would think so too. It has a washing machine, but I'm not sure it works so well. The first week, I put a load of wash in it, pulled the chain, and haven't seen them since.

The weather is great. It only rained twice last week—the first time for three days and the second time for four days.

The coat you wanted is on its way. However, Uncle Benny thought it would cost too much to mail with those big buttons on it, so we cut them off. You can find them in the pockets.

We got locked in Clarence's car yesterday. He spent two hours getting me and Pa out. He couldn't find the keys.

Emma, your sister, had a baby this morning. Funny, that baby is the exact image of your oldest brother Wally. I haven't found out what it is yet. So don't know if you are an aunt or an uncle.

Your poor uncle Willie Joe fell into a whiskey vat last week. They couldn't pull him out, and he burned for two days.

Sorry to tell you this, but four of your friends went off a bridge in a pickup truck. Billie was driving. He and Eddie rolled down the window and swam to safety, but your other two friends drowned. Charlie and Bernie were in the back and couldn't get the tailgate down.

There isn't much more news. Everything is normal around here.

Your favorite aunt,

Mom

Waking Up to a Strange Night

MY HUSBAND HAS BEEN known to do some strange things when sleeping or waking up from a sound sleep.

When we woke up one morning, he proceeded to tell me that he had a really strange dream. He started telling me all about it. He had dreamed that the television wasn't working, and he had worked on it. He had pretty much torn it apart, but he eventually put it back together. He said it really seemed to take a lot of his energy to fix it. I would think so, working on it all night.

We laughed about it but, when we got down to the family room, all the knobs were on top of the TV. When we got the knobs back on, it still worked. One of my husband's trades is an electrician, so he is knowledgeable about such things, but in the middle of the night?

Another time, my husband fell asleep on the couch. I woke him long enough to tell him I was going upstairs to bed. After preparing myself for bed, I heard the downstairs door open and then shut. I heard the door open again and thought he had forgotten something. I heard it happen again, but it sounded like he was slamming it. It happened several more times. Finally, when I heard the door open, I hollered, "What are you doing?"

He hollered back, "I can't find how to turn off the lights."

Laughing, I quickly gave him instructions. When he finally made it upstairs, I was in stitches. He didn't seem to think it was that funny. I guess he was a little embarrassed and upset with himself.

When we went downstairs the next morning, all the electric cords were detached from the walls. They were all over the house. Again, I went into hysterics. I was laughing my head off. Again, he didn't think it was all that funny. Now you understand why I said my husband does some strange things if he has been asleep.

A Trick Pulled on My Sister

MY SISTER AND HER husband lived on a farm in Ohio. Before they had their children, she enjoyed being out with him and helping if she could.

They had several cows, and she would sometimes go out and talk to him while he milked the cows. If she needed to relieve herself, she would just squat over the gutter.

She was in the process of relieving herself one evening, and her husband hollered, "Oh, hi, Meryl." My sister thought her brother in-law was there, and she stood up while pulling up her jeans. She was still in the process and wet all over herself. When she found out he was kidding, she was fit to be tied. For a while, she refused to go out and spend time with him while he was milking the cows. She held that against him for quite some time.

Our family was known for pulling tricks whenever they thought they could get a laugh.

What a Miracle at Christmas

I HAVE NO IDEA WHO wrote this story, but it really struck me as a story everyone would enjoy.

We can all remember taking our kids to the mall to meet Santa and tell him what they wanted for Christmas. This Santa happened to be a very special Santa and was perfect for this job. As you can tell, he really cares for kids.

Three years ago, a little boy and his grandma went to see Santa at a store in Wisconsin. When Kenny's turn came, he climbed up onto Santa's lap.

Santa noticed he had a picture in his hand. "Who is this?"

"My sister Maggie, and she is very sick," he said sadly. "She really loves you and wanted to come and see you so much."

Santa quickly changed the subject, asking, "What is on your list for Christmas?"

As Kenny shared all the things he would like for Christmas, Grandma came over.

Kenny jumped down.

"Is there something you wanted to tell me about Kenny or his sister," Santa asked Grandma.

"This is my granddaughter, and she has a terminal disease. She is not expected to make it through Christmas." Her eyes filled with tears. "Her only wish is to see Santa. Is there any way you could find time to come visit her before Christmas? I know this is a lot to ask of you."

He told the grandmother to leave information with his elves as to where Maggie was. Santa knew what he had to do. *What if it were my child in that hospital bed? I must meet her wish to see Santa.* When it was time to go home, he asked his boss how to get to the hospital where Maggie was.

Rick said, "I'm going too … I'll take you there."

When they arrived at the hospital, they found Maggie's room. Rick waited outside. Santa peeked into the room and saw little Maggie and her family. He recognized the grandma and brother.

Maggie's mother was at her bedside, and an aunt was nearby. They were talking quietly, and Santa could feel the love and concern for Maggie.

Praying for God's help and words, he forced a smile on his face and entered the room, bellowing a hearty, "Ho, ho, ho!"

"Santa!" Maggie forgot how weak she was. With all the wires attached to her body, she couldn't get out of bed to run to him. She was so pale, and her hair had bald patches from the chemotherapy. Her huge, beautiful blue eyes really stood out.

Santa had to force back his tears.

As Maggie talked to Santa, the family gathered around the bed, thanking him and looking sincerely into his eyes. She shared the toys she would love for Christmas, assuring him that she'd been a very good girl that year.

Santa felt the Holy Spirit nudging him to pray for Maggie and asked permission from the girl's mother. She agreed, and the entire family circled around the bed, holding hands.

Santa asked Maggie if she believed in angels.

"Yes, Santa … I do!" she exclaimed.

Placing his hand on the child's head, Santa closed his eyes and prayed. He asked the angels to minister to her and watch and keep her. Next he started singing softly, "Silent night, holy night … all is calm, all is bright."

The whole family, still holding hands, joined in. The nurses and others in the hall did too. Many were crying tears of hope and tears of joy.

When the song ended, Santa said, "Now, Maggie, you have a job to do—and that is to concentrate on getting well."

"Yes, Santa!" Maggie exclaimed.

Santa continued, "I expect to see you at my house at the mall next year!" He knew he was asking much from God, but he had to give her the greatest gift he could. It was not dolls or games or toys. It was the gift of hope. He kissed her on the forehead and left the room. When his eyes met Rick's eyes in the hall, they both wept.

Maggie's mother and grandma rushed out of the room to thank Santa.

"This is the least I could do. I have an eight-year-old myself."

The next year, Santa James was back at the store in Wisconsin.

"Hi, Santa! Remember me?"

"Of course I do," Santa proclaimed (as he always does), smiling down at this beautiful little girl.

"You came to see me in the hospital last year!" she said excitedly.

Santa's heart pumped and tears ran down his cheeks. He jumped up, grabbed this little miracle, and held her tight to his chest. "Maggie!" he exclaimed.

She looked totally different. Her hair was long and silky, and her cheeks were rosy.

Maggie's mother and grandma smiled, waved, and wiped their eyes.

It was the best Christmas for Santa Claus. What a blessing and joy to be a part of bringing about this miracle of hope. This precious little child was totally healed. She was free of that terminal disease—and alive and well.

He silently looked up to heaven and humbly whispered, "Thank you, Father, for another one of your miracles."

It was a very merry Christmas!

Takes Two to Sew

WHEN MY HUSBAND AND I were still living in my father's brick home, we had some pretty cold winters. It was a two-story house, and the upstairs was not heated. In our bedroom, we had plenty of blankets, quilts, socks, and a hot water bottle.

We eventually could afford an electric blanket, which we would heat up before we made a mad dash for the bed. We would put on our nightclothes downstairs. However, it was great for cuddling.

We didn't spend much time on the second floor in the winter. In one of the bedrooms, we had my sewing machine. I would wait until I had several pieces that needed mending before I would go upstairs to do the sewing. The sewing machine was an old-fashioned Singer treadle machine. I was not an accomplished seamstress, and it was very difficult to treadle and guide at the same time to sew a straight seam.

After collecting several items that needed attention, I talked my dear husband into going up there in the cold with me. I was working at it myself, but I was having a terrible time sewing that straight line. We figured out a way that took both of us. Where there is a will, there is a way. He would sit on the chair and treadle, and I would sit on his lap and guide the material to come up with a straight line. It took us a while to get in rhythm since we were both laughing so hard. It was supposed to be work, but we were having so much fun.

When I tried to sew a tie onto my apron, I ended up sewing it to the other end of the tie. That didn't work. We could just imagine what we looked like doing this together. It would look pretty ridiculous. Not too many husbands would have done what he did.

Believe it or not, we got the work done without freezing to death. However, it was a while before we did that again.

A Practical Joke Pulled on Me

IN 1960, FRANK AND I lived in Radnor, Ohio. In that small farming community, the farmers worked hard—but they also liked to have fun by pulling practical jokes on each other.

I came home from work one evening, and as I was passing through the family room, I noticed that the cushions on the living room couch were not the same way I usually placed them. As I looked further, I could see that the couch didn't even belong to us. Someone had been in our house and replaced my custom-made couch with one that was the same color, but it had totally seen its better days.

I panicked for a moment and called my older sister to tell her the situation. We had party line phones back then, and to my surprise, my neighbors were enjoying the joke they had pulled on me. They were laughing. My neighbor was one of the culprits, and the other one was my brother-in law—the husband of my older sister. The neighbor was telling my brother-in-law that he had seen me turning into my home from work.

I was so glad I caught them talking on the phone and didn't make a fool of myself by calling and sharing that someone had been in my home and had stolen my couch. That would have been playing right into their game.

I wondered where my good couch was and found it in the hallway. I'm sure when they started this, they didn't realize how heavy that couch was. It was not an easy task to move it in that narrow hallway. It also was not easy for my husband and other brother-in-law to move it back where it belonged.

I thought about how to handle the situation and decided to call my other sister and ask if they would like to have some fun that night. Being jokers also, they were in for anything.

I suggested that they come over with their truck. We would drop the couch back off in the front yard of my brother-in-law since I knew he was part of the plot. They were all for it, and we decided to bring some gasoline and a lighter to take the old couch home to die.

When we got to their house, they were not home. We knew they liked to play cards at his brother's house and took off for their home. They lived back on a fairly long lane, but we could see their car.

We unloaded the old couch and placed it in the middle of the lane. We poured gasoline on it and lit a match. We blew and blew on the truck horn to get their attention. When they came outside, we took off like a bunch of kids.

That was where the couch came from in the beginning, and so it did go home to die. They couldn't figure out how we knew it came from there.

Their joke backfired because of the party line. We got the last laugh on them!

The Cake Lie

Have you ever told a white lie? Is there such a thing? You are going to love this, especially ladies who bake for church events.

Maggie volunteered to bake a cake for her church ladies' bake sale. She had forgotten about it and thought of it the morning of the sale. After rummaging through her cabinets, she found an angel food cake mix with a past due date, but she didn't have any other choice. She quickly made it while she was drying her hair, dressing, and helping her son pack for camp.

Maggie couldn't wait to see how high the cake had risen. When she opened the oven, the center had fallen flat—and the cake was terribly disfigured. "Now what? There is no time to bake another cake!" Maggie wanted to make a good impression because she was pretty new at the church and wanted to fit in with all the ladies.

She looked around the house for something to build up the center of the cake. She finally ended up in the bathroom. She dropped a roll of toilet paper inside and then covered it with icing. The finished product looked beautiful. It looked perfect. Before she left the house to drop the cake by the church and head for work, Maggie woke her daughter and gave her some money and strict instructions to be at the bake sale the moment it opened at eight thirty to buy the cake and bring it home.

However, when the daughter arrived at the sale, the beautiful cake had already been sold. Misty grabbed her cell phone and called her mom.

Maggie was terrified. She was beside herself! Everyone would know! What would they think? Her reputation would be ruined, talked about, and ridiculed!

All night, Maggie thought about the ladies pointing fingers at her and talking about her behind her back. The next day, Maggie promised not to think about the cake and would attend the fancy luncheon at the home of a fellow church member and try to have a good time.

The hostess was a snob who more than once had looked down her nose at the fact that Maggie was a single parent and not from the elite families of that town. Having already responded that she was coming, she couldn't think of a believable excuse.

The meal was very elegant, and the company was definitely uptown. To Maggie's horror, the cake in question was presented for dessert!

Maggie felt faint when she saw the cake! She started out of her chair to tell the hostess all about it, but before she could get to her feet, the mayor's wife said, "What a beautiful cake!" Maggie, still feeling faint, sat back in her chair.

The hostess, a prominent church member, said, "Thank you. I baked it myself."

Maggie smiled and thought, *God is good*.

Our Special Surprise

FRANK AND I WERE married in 1953 and hoped to start having children in a couple of years. After being married for seven years, the doctors told us that we were not able to have children. We left the office very disappointed and saddened. We went home and shared our situation with our parents. Adoption came up in our conversations, and we quickly decided we definitely wanted children. The next day, we started getting excited about the idea of adopting. We immediately applied for adoption, asking for a newborn.

I was working as a legal secretary. I had told my boss about applying for adoption, and when the time came to receive the baby, I would have to quit immediately because the agency would not allow me to work. Being such a great boss, he said, "No problem. Having a child is far more important than any job. That will be just fine."

Within a month, my husband received a phone call saying they had a newborn daughter for us. We could receive her in five days. Frank called me at work to share the good news. I was so excited and nervous about becoming a mother, especially the whole responsibility of it. I walked into Mr. Jones's office and said, "Mr. Jones, I don't know what to do. I just became a mother."

He said, "Oh, my dear. Do sit down."

After a couple of days of going over things with the new girl, I left my job. Not having anything for a baby, we had much shopping to do for the arrival of our new little surprise. How exciting it was to go shopping and find out all the things that were needed for a little one. We purchased the absolute necessities at first. Later, family and friends gave us a baby shower. How exciting it all was.

The lady from the adoption agency told us to bring them some clothes for her to wear home and a small cardboard box to carry her home in the car—no car seats back then.

Frank and I were so excited and couldn't wait for the time to come. He was staying busy out in the barn, and I decided the time would go faster if I did something to keep me busy. I took out the ironing board and tried to do some ironing. I spent a good part of my time looking down the lane for the lady.

Finally, I saw the dust flying as the lady came driving up the lane. Frank also came running from the barn. She brought our little daughter in the cardboard box all covered over with a baby blanket. She placed the box on the couch, and we quickly and gently pulled the blanket back. She was a beautiful baby girl.

The lady dropped her off and left immediately. We were alone with our baby girl. I guess she thought we could handle it.

When our family and friends found out she had arrived, our home suddenly became filled with people who were as excited as we were. They all showed up to see our precious gift from God. Adoption was rare back then.

We learned very quickly, as most parents do, what it takes to raise a child: lots of work but much joy and love.

This exciting story didn't end there. Thirteen months later, in July 1961, I delivered a boy of our own. In 1968, we had a little girl. What a blessing they have all been. We believe adoption is God's way of sharing those little lives with people who will care for them and love them. What a gift from the natural parents who had to give her up.

Tornadoes or Hurricanes?

In 1963, WE DECIDED we were going to have to spend a lot of money and go really big or get out of farming altogether. The decision to get out was very hard because we had both grown up on farms. Frank had never really done anything else but farm, and he was good at it. He won Young State Farmer of the Year in 1958.

We sold all the farming equipment, livestock, beef cattle, hogs, and household goods.

When I told one of my friends that we were moving to Florida, she said, "Oh, I wouldn't want to live in Florida. I would be afraid of the hurricanes."

I said, "Well, with hurricanes, you know they are coming. You can make plans to take cover or move out of their way. With tornadoes, you have no idea. They come so fast that you don't have time to make plans or get out of their way. I think they are far more dangerous."

Less than two years later, a huge tornado went through several small towns in Ohio. One was Radnor and totally destroyed our brick house. We could have been killed because it took out the whole second floor where we slept, and it happened at night. It destroyed my parents' home (fortunately they were in Florida), my grandparents' home, and my husband's home in Waldo. Many other homes were also destroyed across those small towns—plus several lives.

Sadly, my friend who said she would be afraid of hurricanes and her husband were killed by that tornado. Their son had gone out to check on the dog in the garage, and when he opened the door to go back inside, the house was gone—and so were his parents. He walked across a field to his aunt's house and found out that a large piece of wood had pierced his body. He didn't know it because he was in shock. Thankfully, he lived, but it was just one of the many unfortunate and strange things that happened during the tornado.

My parents would have been killed if they had been home because even the furnace in the basement was a twisted mess. The house was closed up so tightly that it exploded and was completely lost. The piano was found in splinters and pieces in a field. Everything was destroyed, and parts were scattered all over the county. My father's business papers were found in other counties and mailed back to him. My wedding dress was found out in a field covered with mud. Many of their keepsakes, photo albums, business papers, and many other items were gone!

A huge oak tree in their front yard had been uprooted, and my husband's army boots were in the big hole. They were not tied together and had been on a shelf in my parents' basement. It appeared that someone had placed them gently in the hole.

It would take hours to tell all the strange stories that were told in our community. It was sad to have lost some of our friends, but it was a blessing that our family was not hurt.

Homes could be replaced—but lives could not.

What a Hassle

LADIES, CAN ANY OF you relate to this situation? I'll bet something like this has happened to most of us (if we are really honest). Any of us could have written this same story.

When you visit a public bathroom, you will always find a line of women. You smile politely and take your place in the line. When it's finally your turn, and all the doors appear closed, you check for feet under the stall doors. It seems like every one is always occupied. When a door opens, you dash in, barely able to make it.

What's the next issue? The door won't latch. Why do you always seem to get one with this problem? You are about to wet your pants and can't worry about that. Oh, yes. The seat covers up on the wall just happen to always be empty. Oh, well. It's quicker to line the seat with toilet paper anyway. If you are desperate, you just plop your body down on the bare seat.

You look for the hook on the door for your purse or whatever needs to hang there. I was the lucky one to find one with no hook. What would I do with my purse or packages? I draped it over my head and around my neck. There was no way I could place it on the floor after all the preaching Mother had shared over the years about being very careful where you set your purse. She would have turned over in her grave if I had placed it on the bathroom floor.

Finally, you can't worry about anything else. You yank down your pants and assume the stance. When I was younger, this didn't bother me at all, but now I realize some exercise that I have been planning to do for months would have helped at a time like this. You feel your age now, and those muscles begin to shake. You need to sit down, but you didn't take the time to wipe the seat or put down toilet paper. There is nothing else to do but hold the stance. When you're in this position, it goes on a lot longer than usual.

Finally, you reach for the toilet paper dispenser. Of course, it is empty.

I hear Mother saying, "Honey, you should have checked that in the beginning."

Surely, I have a tissue in my purse. I had just cleaned my purse out a few days ago of all those nasty, dirty Kleenex. However, I remembered seeing one tiny tissue this morning that I had used yesterday. That will have to do.

I try not to strangle myself while getting into the purse around my neck. When I finally find the tissue, it is much smaller than I remembered.

Can it get any worse? Someone pushes the door open because the latch doesn't work. The door hits my purse, which is hanging around my neck. I topple back against the tank of the toilet. I'm losing my patience and yell, "Occupied." As I reach to slam the door, I drop my precious tissue in a puddle on the floor.

I lose my balance and fall back. My bottom is now directly in the toilet bowl. I am wet and have no paper. I jump up, knowing it's too late. My bare bottom has made contact with every imaginable germ alive, because I never put down the toilet paper—not that there was any.

What would Mother think of this? I am sure her bare bottom never touched a public toilet seat. I can hear her saying, "You just don't *know* what kind of diseases you can pick up."

Right at that time, the automatic sensor on the back of the toilet flushes, propelling a stream of water like a fire hose against the inside of the bowl. It sprays a fine mist of water that covers my butt and runs down my legs and into my shoes.

The force of the flush sucks everything down. I grab the empty toilet paper dispenser to avoid being dragged in too. At that point, I give up. I'm soaked. I'm exhausted. Fishing into the purse, I only find a gum wrapper.

I slink out inconspicuously to the sinks. It seems like every bathroom has a different type of faucet with automatic sensors. Would you believe I could not get this one to work? I finally worked up some saliva and a dry paper towel and walked past the whole line of waiting women. For some reason, no smile comes to my lips.

A very kind soul at the very end of the line points out a piece of toilet paper trailing from my shoe. Where was that when I needed it? I yank the paper from my shoe, plunk it in the woman's hand, and say, "Here, you just might need this." I continue to exit.

Standing there with a very annoyed look on his face is your hubby. "What took you so long—and why is your purse hanging around your neck?"

Restrooms! (Rest?) you've got to be kidding!

This is why men never have to stand in line. It also answers the other commonly asked questions about why women go to the restroom in pairs. It's so the other gal can hold the door, hang onto your purse, and hand you Kleenex under the door!

Fishing with Daddy

MY PARENTS WERE FARMERS for more than forty years and spent the winters in Florida for several years. After my husband and I got married—and he had served in the army for two years—we started farming for my father.

In the winter, the demands of the farm were minimal. We were able to take a few weeks to visit them in Florida.

My father loved to fish, and I guess that was the main reason why they loved to go to Florida. They also had some relatives who lived there. I guess I took after my father because I love to go fishing. I didn't care much whether we caught any fish or not. I just loved the quietness of the water, and we would pack plenty of food for lunch and for snacks throughout the day.

One day, there were five of us in the boat: my dad, myself, my two sisters—one who lived in Florida and the other who was also visiting from Ohio—and my nephew, who was around twelve years old.

We were fishing in the port at Cape Canaveral, where the Kennedy Space Center is located. We were able to catch tripletail fish quite often in that area. They were so much fun to catch because we reeled them in—and then they would take off. We had to repeat the procedure many times before we finally wore them down and could bring them into the boat.

The day was unbelievable. They must have been hungry because we all had one on our line at the same time. We had to go under and over each other in order not to get our lines tangled. We were having so much fun, and all of us were dying laughing. My dad was enjoying us having such a great time. We reeled in all five! They can be very large fish. They all were in the range of fifteen to twenty-two pounds. They were delicious.

Daddy was very good at sharing them. He would go to the poorer sections of Cocoa, Florida, and share with the people there. They loved to see Daddy show up, and he would do it quite often.

Another time, Daddy and my husband went out to fish around some channel markers that led to deeper water. My husband was sitting at the bow of the boat, and he spotted a large shadow in the water. He asked my father what it could be. My father immediately shouted to pull up the stringer of trout that they had already caught in the port.

As my husband quickly pulled it in, he noticed the shadow was approaching the boat. A huge hammerhead shark was headed for the boat where the stringer of trout had been hanging. It went directly under their boat. It was longer than the boat, and my husband almost could have touched it. As it passed under the rear of the boat, my father poked it with his fishing pole. My husband yelled, "Don't make it angry at us!"

It could have easily upset the boat. My father quickly pulled in the anchor, started the boat, and motored it back to the port. They were both very happy to be back in safe waters. They talked about that scary incident for years. It made quite a mark on their lives, knowing God's angels were protecting them again.

Hitchhikers Welcome

BACK IN THE EIGHTIES, my husband loved to pick up hitchhikers. Most of them were from other countries. Back then, you rarely heard about any problems with hitchhikers.

He would often bring them home for dinner. We sometimes had to tell the family to go easy and allow more for the hitchhiker. We didn't allow them to stay overnight because we had three young children.

One day, I hadn't been home all day and didn't have dinner prepared. My husband brought home two young hitchhikers from Switzerland. We took our family and the two boys to a buffet restaurant. I never saw two boys put away more food. They went back and forth to that buffet many times. I don't remember if they had ever been to one before. We were so thrilled that they were enjoying the meal so much.

When my husband picked them up, he asked where they were from and where they were going. When he found out they were from Berne, he got very interested because that is where his ancestors came from. My husband introduced himself and said his last name was Howald. The boys looked at each other, and the one boy who could speak better English pointed to his friend and said, "He is a Howald." They could have very well been related! They started talking about people in their past.

They were very nice boys, and we did allow them to spend the night on our screened-in back porch. The next day, my husband drove them as far as he could toward their next destination on his way to work.

In our many experiences with hitchhikers, we had never received a card or a thank-you note. We received a very nice postcard from them. They invited us to visit, and we could stay free in the family's hotel in Berne. We never got to go, but we had been there in the fifties when my husband was in the army.

My husband loved to do this for hitchhikers, and he always talked to them about their relationships with God. It was amazing how many of them were familiar with the Lord.

It is sad that it is not always safe to pick up hitchhikers these days. It is very hard for my husband to pass them by because he made many nice acquaintances through the years.

Dinner and a Scarf

WHEN WE WERE ATTENDING a church in Frontenac, Florida, we met a young woman who was a bit slow and a little disabled.

I tried to show her love, and she took a real liking to me. She invited my husband and me to dinner. She lived in a little apartment close to the church. We didn't know what to expect, but we thought it was right to accept her invitation.

When we arrived, she nicely offered us coffee. We kindly agreed to have a cup. We both took a sip and looked at each other. It actually tasted like dishwater. While she was in the kitchen, my husband opened the front door and tossed his into the bushes.

I said, "Thanks a lot. What am I supposed to do with mine?"

He was able to open the door and tossed mine into the bushes too. We hoped the bushes would survive. We were wondering if we should have accepted dinner if it was like the coffee, but it was too late to back out.

When she called us to the table, we weren't sure what she was serving. When we finished, we were asking each other if it was pork or chicken. The rest of the meal was a little questionable also, but we got through it. I really loved her and knew it was something she did because she really loved my husband and me.

When Christmas came, she told me she had a gift for me. On Sunday, she was all excited about it. When I got it home and opened it, we weren't quite sure what it was. The crocheted scarf (we thought) was about four inches wide and approximately six feet long. A note was pinned to it that said: "Oops. Sorry—accidently spilled some coffee, and it made a stain." I loved it!

A Close Call for My Husband

MY HUSBAND WAS DRIVING his truck to work one morning. He was stopped at a stoplight, and the light turned green. He went to step on the gas, but the truck decided to die. He couldn't figure why the truck decided to die at that moment. A car came speeding through the light, and if the truck had not died, he would have been smack dab in the path of that car, which was going way over the speed limit.

We don't always understand why things happen the way they do, but we need to give more credit to God when some of these strange things happen. God has His angels watching over us, and we need to stop and think before we complain and get angry. My husband had much to be thankful for that morning. After the car went through the light, the truck performed perfectly. Thank you, God, for our guardian angels.

A Lost Boat Motor

OUR SON AND HIS friend lived on our street in Cocoa. It was only one block from the Indian River, and they enjoyed going out in our Gheenoe (a canoe with a flat back to hold a small outboard motor).

They were enjoying their ride and decided it was time to turn around and head back to shore. Our son turned the motor to a ninety-degree angle, and because the motor was not secured correctly, it flipped up and out of the water (which was dangerous) and disappeared into the water. Our son was smart and quick enough to drop the anchor so it would be in the vicinity of where the motor was.

When my husband arrived home from work, the two boys excitedly shared the experience with him. My husband put on his bathing suit and went down to the river with the boys to see if they could locate the motor. The water was only chest deep, and they were hoping they would stumble upon it. They spent quite some time doing just that. That didn't work, and they had to come up with another plan.

After thinking about what else they could do, my husband came up with the idea of using a long pipe with ropes attached to each end and then bringing them together with him pulling the system. People driving along the river road were wondering what this man was doing walking back and forth in the river with the ropes over his shoulder. Cars were driving slowly, and some almost stopped.

My husband doesn't give up easily. Eventually, he felt the pipe strike the motor. We are sure God was in the picture from beginning to end. The motor was restored, the boys were not hurt, and they probably learned a lesson.

Hitchhikers' Story

I HAVE ALREADY MENTIONED THAT my husband loved to pick up hitchhikers and always talked to them about the Lord. He usually started out asking them if they were Christians. This man happened to be a Christian and proceeded to tell my husband the following story of what happened in his life.

His life was not one to be proud of. He did most of the things that are not good for your health and for your everyday life. He dealt with drugs, alcohol, and girls. You name it—he was guilty. Because of this, he had lost his family. He was leading a life of depression and had other problems.

He had come home one night already drunk and decided to turn on the TV and have another drink before going to bed. During this time, he passed out on the floor. When he finally came to, the TV was on the 700 Club, a Christian station that is still on the air today. This big, good-looking black man was talking about salvation. It was as if this man was speaking directly to him and pointing his finger right at him. He was going on about how his life needed to change and that the Lord Jesus Christ could help. This man even told him not to touch the dial. He made the decision to accept the Lord in his life, and his life was never the same. He never touched another drink and had no desire to do so. He was able to get his family back, but he needed to find a good job to provide for them. They were living in a motel.

He was on his way back to Titusville from interviewing for a job in Rockledge, Florida, when my husband picked him up. My husband gave this man some money before he dropped him off. This man got out of the van, and my husband watched him run and then jump and run and then jump. It was such a blessing to my husband to see this man so excited and happy because he had some money to help feed his family.

We were in Amway at that time, and this big, good-looking man named Ben was the speaker at one of the rallies. After he finished speaking, my husband found him and told him this story. He was so happy to hear the story because he had been deciding whether to stay with the 700 Club or change to another ministry. He wasn't sure he was reaching people like he wanted to. He told my husband that was confirmation that he was to stay where he was on the 700 Club.

We never know how our stories or sharing someone else's story can touch lives. That is what I am hoping for by writing this book.

Tragedy at the Rodeo

OUR FAMILY WAS LOOKING for something to do one Sunday afternoon after church. We decided to go to the rodeo in Kissimmee, Florida. It was only about fifty miles from our home.

We took our three children plus two of our friends' boys. Their father was the superintendent of Fairglen Elementary School where our children attended school.

The place was pretty packed, but we were able to find a parking place not too far from the stadium. We got the kids some drinks and food and settled in the bleachers.

We were enjoying the different acts when we noticed smoke way out in the field. Lots of large coaches and beautiful cars were parked there. We kept our eyes on it, and suddenly a large coach blew up. We then watched another coach blow and then another. Cars and trucks also caught fire. There were probably ten or fifteen vehicles on fire. We figured it was probably people in the rodeo who had so many coaches. Several fire engines showed up and got the situation under control.

We kept wondering why they didn't announce something about it, but then we decided they didn't want to cause a panic during the show.

My husband said it was probably the catalytic converter in a car parked in the tall grass. We were so thankful we didn't decide to park in the fields around the rodeo.

They finally announced that the insurance company was in the office. People could talk to them if their vehicles were damaged. We were so sorry about the fires and the people's losses, but we still enjoyed the fun we had at the rodeo. It was exciting for us but sad for others.

Can You Top This One?

I THINK THERE IS ONE of these in most churches and businesses. It keeps life from getting too boring, especially if there is a "Herbert" close by. He was a man of few words, but his brain was always working.

Mildred was known in the church for talking too much. She could see everyone else's faults, but she had trouble seeing her own. She was known as the church gossip—as much as I hate saying that about someone. Many in the church did not approve of her extra activities, but they never brought them up for fear she would find something to share with others about them. She had a way of making things a little juicier than they actually were.

She didn't know Herbert very well since he was a new member in the church. Messing with Herbert was probably her biggest mistake. She accused him of being an alcoholic. She had seen his pickup parked in front of the only bar in a little country town the day before. She informed him—and everyone else she met up with in that small community—that they knew what he was doing at that bar. Assumption can sometimes be a sin.

When Mildred accused Herbert of being an alcoholic, he stared at her for a moment, turned, and walked away. More of us should follow Herbert's reaction to Mildred's accusations. He didn't explain, defend, or deny it. He said nothing.

An idea popped into Herbert's mind. Later that evening, Herbert quietly parked his pickup in front of Mildred's house, walked home, and left it there all night.

You gotta love Herbert! He may have been a man of few words, but he knew how to shut up a woman.

What You Don't Know Doesn't Hurt You

Churches receive many people who stop in for help. They ask for gas, food, a place to stay, and many other things.

We were at church one evening when a car pulled in and asked for help. They had four children in the car. One was a two-year-old with only one leg, and they also had animals. Another couple happened to be going into church when these people drove up. My husband was a deacon and decided that they really needed help. They didn't appear to have drinking or drug problems, so we and the other couple were willing to help them.

We skipped church to serve them and took them to a motel down the road. We purchased food and took it to them. We took several loads of their clothes to the Laundromat. We dumped the clothes out on the floor and tried to sort them into color piles without making too much contact. Our husbands told us later that they saw all these fleas come out of the clothes when we dumped them out. Fortunately, the women didn't see it. Otherwise, we would have been done really quick and they could have finished the job.

When we started taking the clothes out of the dryer little droppings showed up. Apparently, the diapers had not been cleaned out. We didn't notice that when we were handling them. We quickly turned that situation over to our husbands because someone had to clean out the dryer before we could put anything else in it. We gals weren't up to that.

We tried to decide if we should wash them over, but we decided they were at least better than they had been before. We had several loads and needed to get them back to the family.

When we took them back to the motel, the walls in the shower were almost black from all the showers they had taken. We felt we had done all we could do for them. We prayed for them and asked God to help them, especially the two-year-old. We quickly headed back to the church.

We never know what the Lord will require of us. We just have to be willing and ready to serve Him and others.

Letting Go of Our Son

OUR SON WAS ALWAYS a little on the shy side. Even when he was in middle school, he wouldn't go into a 7-Eleven to get a gallon of milk for us.

When the time came for him to graduate, we started talking about college. Where did he want to go to college? How was he going to get along since he was so quiet and shy? My husband's sister had gone to a college in Longview, Texas. LeTourneau was a Christian engineering college.

We took a trip to Texas to check it out, and he decided he wanted to go there. After returning home and giving it more thought, he applied and was accepted.

On our trip to take our son to school, we stopped at a restaurant. After he took quite a long time deciding what he was going to order, he came up with the most unusual meal on the menu. We had no idea what it was. We asked him what it was, and he said, "I have no idea what it is, but I will have to eat whatever the cafeteria serves when I get to school. I decided I might as well start now!" After being so particular at home, he ate every bit of whatever it was.

After arriving at school and getting everything unpacked and his room set up, it was time for us to leave. After we said our goodbyes and drove away, I immediately started crying. Our son looked so lonely as he waved goodbye to us.

I said, "How is he going to get along since he is so quiet and reserved?"

We agreed that we had to put him in the hands of the Lord. He would take care of our son. However, I still cried all the way home.

After we left, he had to go to the auditorium for orientation. When he walked in, groups of kids were standing around and talking. He noticed one group and decided he would be brave and see if he could join them. That group of boys ended up being his best friends all through college. They came to our house in Florida for spring break and were in his wedding. God honored our prayer when we put him in the hands of God. God is so good!

During the summer, he worked for his father at the Kennedy Space Center. He proved himself to be a good worker, and his father told him he had to work harder than anyone because he was his son. Because of their close relationship during that summer, when it came time for our son to go back to college, my husband was the one who teared up. I felt fine because I knew he and God could make it through together.

No Identification

ON MERRITT ISLAND, A neighbor who was an Amway distributor shared the opportunity with us. It sounded like fun, and we decided to give it a try.

Over the years, we were able to build a fairly large business. Amway is very good about rewarding you if you work hard and do the work it takes. We made it to the first step of rewards and were given a free trip to Hawaii.

The morning we were to leave, I was getting the last-minute things together. I decided to leave my billfold at home so my purse would be a lot lighter. Everything was being paid for, and my husband had any money we would need in his billfold. I took it out and left it on a shelf in my closet.

After arriving in Orlando, we had to go through the lines and show identification at the ticket counter. Oh no—my billfold had all my identification in it. They informed me that I had to have a picture ID in order to board the plane. My husband never gets too upset with me and has a good right to many times. That would have been an appropriate time, but he merely said, "What are we going to do?"

We were plenty early and decided we had time to call our oldest daughter who was at work. She would race over to our house, grab the billfold, and bring it to the airport, which was an hour away from our home. Bless her boss. He allowed her to make the trip. Thankfully, she had a key to our house. She found the billfold and raced to the airport. We met her outside. She had her arm out the window with the billfold in it, and we grabbed it and ran. We found out later she was driving eighty miles an hour all the way in order to get it to us on time. Thankfully, God protected her. We were praying for her safety.

We ran inside and opened the billfold, but my license was not there. I remembered that I had taken the license out for an unknown reason. It was actually in another purse. Oh no. What were we going to do?

I went over to the counter and told the lady what we had done. I showed her that my license was missing, but I had a voter card and credit cards. Nothing had my picture on it. She kept saying that they had to have a picture.

They started moving me to another person and then another. Finally, a lady had mercy on me. I think she was just glad to get rid of us. She finally said, "Oh well. Go on."

We raced out to the plane, which was actually waiting on us to board. As we entered the plane, we received a big round of applause. Most of them were business people.

It was a good lesson for me. I always make sure I have my billfold when I go on any kind of a trip, especially flying. I also bring another picture ID. They warned me that I might have the same problem when boarding the plane to come home. Thankfully, I was never asked for any identification while in Hawaii or on the plane coming home.

We had a wonderful trip. I would love to go back and have some more of that delicious pineapple. We went on excursions, rented a convertible, and rode around the island with another couple in our business. What a blessing it was to us!

The Bizarre Christmas Bazaar

SOME OF MY FRIENDS and I went to a Christmas bazaar at a lady's home. Many ladies went and sold their goodies there. Some had done it for several years. We always enjoyed it, and they always had beautiful things for sale. It was mostly things they had made during the year.

At the bazaar, there were beautiful arrangements, wreaths, wall and table decorations, and Christmas tree decorations. We almost always found new and interesting things for our homes.

We were walking through the different rooms and sharing our comments about the many lovely things when I noticed someone's heel on the carpet. I said, "Oh my goodness. Someone lost a heel. I'll just put it here on this table. Maybe someone will claim it."

I started noticing little pieces of stuff here and there on the carpets and in the different rooms. I didn't know what it was, and I didn't really think much more about it. It seemed to be all over the place.

We purchased some items and went outside. As soon as my feet hit the sidewalk, I realized I was walking funny.

I looked down—and I was the one missing my heel. We all started laughing so hard. I was the one leaving all the stuff on the floor. My shoes were literally falling apart. My sandals had some years on them, and I hadn't worn them for a long time. They actually had dry rot. The cork was crumbling all over the carpets. How embarrassing! We laughed so hard we almost … well, you know what happens when women do too much laughing. We almost did!

We had planned on doing more shopping after leaving the bazaar, but I couldn't walk around with my heel missing. I really didn't want to buy a pair of new shoes since my closet was full of shoes. We stopped by an army-navy store, and I purchased a cheap pair of sneakers.

A couple of weeks later, my granddaughter visited. As we were getting ready for church, she asked if she could wear a pair of my sandals. I said, "Sure. Help yourself."

She volunteered at a nursery and noticed there was stuff all over the floors. She remembered my story and looked at her shoes. The soles were crumbling everywhere. She didn't want them to know she was making the mess and quietly excused herself. Again, we had a good laugh over Grammy's shoes. When I had time, I went through my shoes and decided it was time to part with a few.

College Antics

OUR SON WAS ATTENDING a Christian engineering college in Longview, Texas, and he decided to have some fun on Halloween. One of his friends went to bed early, and he and two other close friends decided to pull a trick on him.

A newspaper company was close by. They decided it would be fun to fill their friend's car with newspapers. Halloween was a good time for a trick. The dumpsters behind the newspaper company were always full of reams of paper. Since they had no ink on them, they wouldn't ruin his car.

My son took the keys from the friend's dresser, and he and his other friends started on their mission. Everything was going well. They made several trips to the dumpster and filled up the car.

As they were walking down the alley to get one last batch of paper, a white Cadillac came squealing down the alley at them. The boys decided to run. The car followed them. It ran over curbs, across driveways, and through a vacant lot. The boys agreed to stop because a man in a cowboy hat was holding a gun out of the window of his car. They found out later he was going to a Halloween party.

When the man got out of his car, he pointed the gun straight at them. It was very scary and unusual since they had always been straight kids. That's when they suspected that the man was an undercover policeman.

The policeman asked them what they were doing. The boys told him they were just having some fun and pulling a trick on their school buddy. As they were talking, the policeman's car started rolling forward. It was picking up speed. He had forgotten to put it in park or set the emergency brake. He was on a slight downgrade. The policeman had his back to his car and didn't see it. The boys started pointing to the car, but the policeman thought they were trying to distract him. They finally said, "Sir, your car is moving." He turned and took off running after his car.

The boys took that opportunity to run back to the dorm.

They thought they had enough excitement for one night. The Lord had taken care of them by allowing the runaway police car to take priority over the situation. God looks out for His kids.

A Great Comeback

I LOVED HOW CHARLIE ANSWERED the question sent to the little town newspaper, and I think you'll love it too.

The Gazette received a very interesting letter from a churchgoer named George. He was known for complaining about anything and everything. He thrived on thinking he was always right. This time, he was complaining that it didn't make any sense to him to go to church every Sunday. He said, "I've been going to church for probably about twenty years now. I've heard around two thousand sermons, and I can't remember a single one. I decided the pastors are wasting their time—and the people's time too."

Maybe George wasn't listening and was trying to think of something to complain about.

Our small community was mostly Christians, and it did not go down too well. The people had a hard time swallowing his garbage.

His letter really got the attention of the people in the town. The newspaper had never received so much mail. It was pouring in. After several days, they received a great letter from Charlie. He had lived in the community for years. He was also a churchgoer, but maybe he was one who did listen. The letter did not go down well with him, and he let George know about it.

Charlie said, "George, I have a little something to say for you to think about. I have been married to my beautiful wife for more than twenty years. Sarah cooks me three meals a day.

Were they good? Yes, I do remember that. Do I remember what they were? Heavens no. It probably adds up to more than twenty-two thousand meals. For the life of me, I cannot recall the entire menu for a single one of those meals—and my wife doesn't expect me too. However, I do know this: they gave me the nourishment and strength I needed to do my work. If Sarah had not given me those meals, I would be physically dead today. Likewise, if I had not gone to church for nourishment, I would be spiritually dead today!"

It was a great comeback from Charlie! Thank God for our physical and spiritual nourishment!

Scottsdale, Arizona

WE LOVED BEING AMWAY distributors. We were always treated like royalty with the best hotels, wonderful speakers, terrific food, and great rewards for our work.

For our hard work, we won a free trip to Scottsdale, Arizona. We were offered several excursions there. One of the excursions was a hot-air balloon ride. We decided on that one. Even though I was afraid of heights, it was too good an opportunity not to take advantage of.

There were two other couples and a pilot in the fairly small basket. It was so much fun. I was not scared at all. It didn't seem like we were up that high, and we felt very safe and at ease. There were many other balloons in the area.

We were enjoying the ride, and we could see rabbits and other animals running around below us. Then we started spinning very slowly. I thought, *Wow! This is so much fun.* We started spinning a little faster, and then faster, and then we were swinging way out. We began to wonder whether we were supposed to be doing that. We were in what they called a toilet bowl. It was a very dangerous thing. Being so close to the other balloons, we could have had a collision. Our pilot never said anything until the flight was over. Thankfully, he was able to get control of it again and stopped the spinning. He didn't want us to be afraid and kept it all to himself, which was very smart of him. We really did have a wonderful time, and if I had the opportunity again, I would go.

It was very interesting how they rolled it out and inflated it with a gas burner that filled it with the hot air. We waited for the balloon to rise up above the basket, which was anchored down, and were able to get in the basket. As the balloon got larger and larger, it lifted us off the ground. Away we went—up, up, and away. As we traveled on our journey, a chaser truck followed us so they would know where we landed. It was interesting how they deflated it and rolled it up to take back to where we started. A lot of work went into that.

A friend of ours took hot-air balloon lessons in Tennessee. When she went to take her solo flight to get her license, it was a little windy. She should have waited for another day, but she was anxious to get it over with.

She went ahead and took the ride. Her instructor told her to stay out of the fields where the cows were since they were private property. When it was time for her to bring it down, she couldn't control it. The wind was getting stronger and was blowing her into areas she didn't want to go. If I remember right, she was up there for several hours. She was beginning to panic. She was afraid of running out of gas and was exhausted.

Because the wind wasn't cooperating, she eventually ran out of gas. She landed in an area where there were trees and fences that damaged the balloon. Thankfully, she was not hurt. However, she still landed in a field where there were cows! I don't think the cows minded, but maybe the instructor and the owner did. She did get her license.

Living Close to the Space Center

WHEN WE LIVED ON Merritt Island, my husband was part owner of a construction company. They performed construction, electrical, and general contracts at the Kennedy Space Center in Cape Canaveral.

We were very familiar with all the different vehicle launches. We could view them from our front yard. Having seen so many go up, we knew how they were supposed to perform. The early stages included the separation of the solid rocket boosters from the main core of the vehicle. We knew how they would fall away.

On the morning of the *Challenger* launch in 1986, I was watching the countdown on TV, anxiously waiting to see it go up.

I was especially interested in that flight because my brother, a teacher, had applied to be chosen for the mission. He was disappointed that he wasn't chosen.

After viewing the initial liftoff on TV, I dashed to the front yard to see it as it started its mission. As I watched, it appeared to perform normally up until the solid boosters fell away. At that point, everything changed. It looked like an explosion, and many pieces were falling from the sky. I thought, *This is not normal. I think it blew up.* I ran back into the house to see what they were saying on TV. The news was not good. They were announcing that it had blown up.

It was so devastating to hear the news, thinking of all the astronauts who had lost their lives. I felt sorry for the teacher, but I was thankful that my brother wasn't on that mission.

We need to be more thankful for people that put themselves in harm's way for the scientific purpose of learning more about God's world.

Not Grandma and Grandpa— Grammy and Grampy

WHEN OUR SON AND daughter-in-law were going to have our first grandchild, they wanted to know what we wanted to be called. We said, "Grandma and Grandpa would be fine."

When our granddaughter was about four years old, she was not a big talker. I was trying to get her to come to me.

She stopped, put her little hands on her hips, and said, "You not Grandma."

I thought, *Oh dear. What have I done to make her say that?* I said, "Well, if I'm not Grandma, who am I?"

She had the cutest little grin on her face as she was thinking. She finally said, "You Grammy."

I said, "Well, if I'm Grammy, who is Grandpa?"

She thought again, and she said, "He's Grampy."

I looked at her mother and said, "Did that come from you?"

She shook her head and said, "I have no idea where that came from."

I loved it that she had come up with names for us rather than us naming ourselves. We now have eleven grandchildren and seven great-grandchildren. We are Grammy and Grampy to all of them. Those names are especially precious to us because our first grandchild preferred those names to Grandma and Grandpa.

Miracle Rest Area

MY HUSBAND AND I went on a trip with my daughter and her family. As we were nearing home, we knew that the next rest area was the last one before we arrived home. We decided to stop.

It took a while since there were several of us plus two children and two dogs. When we took off, we were looking forward to being home again.

When we arrived home about forty-five minutes later, we all piled out. Where were the dogs? Oh no. We were missing the dogs. They were usually the first to jump out. Where were the dogs? We all looked at each other, thinking the same thing. They must have snuck out of the van at the rest area—and we didn't notice. Panic set in. What do we do?

The decision was made that my husband and daughter would race back to the rest area to see if they were still running around there and looking for their family.

They returned home with no success. However, the manager at the rest area suggested calling the police and animal control to see if they had been contacted by someone who had found them. She called both places and left her phone number. At that time, they knew nothing about the dogs. In the meantime, we had been praying and asking the Lord to help us find those precious little miniature dachshunds.

Early the next day, by the grace of God, the phone rang. A lady was calling about the dogs. They were leaving the rest area when they saw two little dogs running toward the highway. They pulled over, and the dogs were willing to jump into the car with no problems. The amazing part of the story is that they lived in Cocoa, which was just across the bridge—only about ten miles.

My daughter and I went to pick up the dogs. They were cuddled up on the bed, enjoying their little episode. However, they were very happy to see us. The nice people would take no reward of any kind. They just loved dogs and were happy to be a part of the miracle of the dogs finding their family again.

Whenever we pass that rest area, we think back about what a miracle it was that we found the dogs only ten miles away. It could have been Miami or some other state. God knows how much we love our animals—just like we know how much He loves us.

When we are traveling past that rest stop, we say, "There's the miracle rest area."

Saving Our Granddaughter

OUR FAMILY WAS HAVING a gathering at my brother's home. We had just finished eating (we always have to eat) and were seated on the porch. Do you know the old wives' tale to not go swimming too soon after you eat because you might get cramps? Maybe they said it so the parents could relax from the full meal and not have the responsibility of keeping their eye on the kids in the pool.

The little ones had been told this story and had to wait a while before going in the pool. We weren't paying any attention to the pool. Our oldest granddaughter was only four and asked her mother why another granddaughter who was only two could go into the pool when she and her sister couldn't. This quickly got the attention of her mother. The little two-year-old (their cousin) had fallen in while reaching for a floating toy. Our daughter-in-law took action, quickly jumping into the pool to rescue her.

The rest of us didn't know the little one had fallen into the pool and were wondering why our daughter-in-law was jumping into the pool with her clothes on. When she lifted our little granddaughter out of the water, we all looked at each other. We quickly helped them out of the pool. The little one was fine and had not been in there very long before her cousin noticed.

It brought to mind how other children have drowned when there are too many people around. Everyone thinks someone else is watching the children. When there is a pool, pond, or river close to where there are children, we always have to be alert. Children are so quick, and we can lose them in an instant.

We are very grateful that the Lord brought the older granddaughter's attention to that situation.

A Water Park in Orlando

SEVERAL YEARS AGO, MY son, his wife, and their five children went with us to a water park in Orlando. I put on my bathing suit, but I planned on only being an onlooker.

We walked into the park and saw a big water slide. Everyone else was oohing and aahing over it. They were all prepared to go on the water slide. After they all tried it a couple of times, they started coaxing me to go. They shared that MeMom (their other grandmother) had gone, and she didn't get her hair wet. They said, "Come on, Grammy. You will like it—and you don't have to get your hair wet."

They told me my head wouldn't go under. "That is what MeMom did, and she didn't get her hair wet." I didn't want to be outdone by the other grandmother, and I finally gave in. I believed what they had told me. When I went down the slide, the tube went one way—and I went the other way. My glasses flew off. I came up fluttering and sputtering. I looked up at my family, and they all had their mouths wide open. They couldn't believe what had happened to Grammy.

The lady in charge found my glasses at the other end of the pool. They were unharmed. I don't know why I didn't remove my glasses first. Oh, yes. I remember now. I wasn't going to go underwater. My glasses would be fine!

The rest of the day, I felt like a drowned rat. I didn't have much makeup on, but my eye makeup was smeared. However, as I looked around, there seemed to be other people in the same condition as me. I decided not to worry about it and enjoy the day. Those are the things that make memories. It is fun to bring them up later in life.

A Tragic Accident

WHEN MY DAUGHTER AND her husband were attending college in Tulsa, Oklahoma, they would come back home to Florida. They would drive straight through the night. They weren't blessed with much money during that time and found it was much cheaper to keep driving.

My daughter was driving, and my son-in-law was sleeping. All of a sudden, he awoke and said, "Slow down. Something doesn't look right up ahead."

She listened and slowed down. It was very dark. When they got close enough, they could see a semi had overturned, and the bottom of the truck was facing them. That's why it looked so dark.

Another car had already plowed into the truck, and the passengers were tragically killed. My kids quickly parked in a safe place and tried to flag down another car, but they wouldn't stop and plowed into the truck. They quickly called 911 and went to help the people. They were badly hurt. They continued flagging down other cars.

The police finally came, and the kids were able to go to the first rest area to wash up. They felt they had done all they could do except pray for these people.

They especially took time to pray to God to thank Him for waking my son-in-law just in time or they could have been one of those cars in the tragic accident. God is so good and looks out after His children.

Retirement Is Not All It Is Cracked up to Be

After Christmas break, Miss Thomas asked her young students to write a story about how they spent their vacations. These were always quite interesting and entertaining. She especially enjoyed the little boy who visited his grandpa and grandma who used to live on a farm. His story:

"We used to spend Christmas with Grandma and Grandpa. They lived on a big farm in the country, and we always had lots of fun with the animals and riding the tractor. It is hard work, and I guess all that farm work made them have to move to Florida.

"Now they live in this funny tin box that sits on wheels. They don't have grass, but they painted the rocks green to look like grass. Grandma and Grandpa both have bikes and ride all over the place. There are a lot of tin boxes where other people live. It is funny how they have to wear tags with their names on them because they don't always know who they are anymore. Their bikes also have flags on them so people won't run over them.

"They have a room there called the 'wrecked center.' I guess they must have had someone fix it because it didn't look wrecked to me. They go there almost every day. They have a lot of other friends who also go there, and they play all kinds of games and things. They meet other people like themselves and do exercises. They are funny and not anything like my dad. There is a swimming pool too, but it is also funny. They all just jump up and down with these funny hats on.

"My favorite place is this cute little dollhouse at the front gate. A cute little old man just sits in it all day. I guess his job is not to let anyone go in or out because they might forget where *this* is or how to get back in. Sometimes a few people sneak out when he is not looking in their golf carts. If the people make it out, they can bring back food and eat it at the wrecked center. Grandma told me they call it potluck.

"Grandma was a good cook and used to cook good things for us to eat. I guess she forgot how. I think she is the same as Grandpa. They eat out every day, and they always eat the same thing. They are early birds.

"Grandpa and Grandma kept telling me how important it was for me to work hard so I could retire like them someday. When I'm retired, I want to be the little old man in the dollhouse. I know I will let them out so they can go visit their grandchildren."

The Good and the Bad of the Move

OUR DAUGHTER AND SON-IN-LAW were in the process of moving back to Florida from Virginia. He was changing jobs. We had driven out to help our daughter and their two children pack up and move. Our son-in-law was already working in Florida.

While we were in Virginia, the news was talking about a sniper on the loose in the area where they lived. They had to be careful if they went anywhere. He was shooting on the highway, outside of malls, and in many other places. People were not safe anywhere.

When my daughter and I would go out, we would run to the store in a zigzag fashion as they had told us to do. It was a very crazy and scary time because a number of people had been shot. Our husbands appreciated our fear of going out to run errands (or shopping) since it was much better on their billfolds.

After we left Virginia, the snipers were finally captured. One was killed, and the other ended up in prison.

Our trip to Virginia was filled with good times in anticipation of their move back, but we had to endure the fear of what was going on all around us while we were there. However, we were blessed with God's protection and felt thankful when the evil was over for that area.

Another Blessing

I HAVE SO MANY STORIES about how God has helped me find jewelry that I thought I had lost. He has performed many miracles for me, but many are about jewelry. I know it is because He knows how much I enjoy wearing jewelry. I don't worship it, but I enjoy it.

When we visited Texas, we heard about a famous jewelry store. We happened to run into it in one of the big malls. Many of the pieces had Christian symbols on them. They had gold and silver, and we could usually get the same piece in either color.

I purchased a couple of beautiful gold rings. One was a pinkie ring with a gold cross dangling from it. The first one I purchased was silver. We had a friend whose daughter was dying of cancer. She was just a young lady. She admired my ring, and I decided to give it to her. She seemed to enjoy it, but she didn't live too long to enjoy it.

When I had the opportunity, I was able to purchase one in gold. While wearing it one day, I noticed the little cross was gone. I was really disappointed because I really enjoyed that ring. It brought on many conversations with others who were admiring it.

I prayed that God would help me find that ring. Otherwise, I would have to send my ring to Texas to get it repaired. That little cross was quite expensive.

A few days later, I happened to see something on the throw rug in front of the kitchen sink. I reached down, and it was my beautiful little cross. I was able to take it to a jewelry store and get it welded back on. I know that cross could have been anywhere, but God brought my attention to it right in my own home where I could find it. God has so much love for us and enjoys blessing us.

Another time, I lost a gold bracelet. I had no idea where it was. About a year later, my husband was doing a deep cleaning in our car. He was looking for something he had lost. Way down deep in the seat area, he found my gold bracelet. I had finally given up and forgotten about it, but my dear Lord hadn't forgotten or given up on us finding it. He finally got our attention to look deep in the car, and we would find something we had been looking for.

We had an opportunity to go to New Jersey to visit our son-in-law's family. I always take my rings off at night. I thought I put them all on top of the chest. When I went to put my rings on the next day, they were all there—except for my little pinkie ring. We looked high and low for that ring. When we left, we said, "Don't worry about it. If it shows up, let us know. It has to be somewhere, and only God knows right now."

A few months later, I went to put on the boots I had worn to New Jersey. As I picked one up, it sounded like something made a noise inside. As I turned it upside down, my little gold pinkie ring fell out. God had it safe all the time and knew I would find it eventually. I know there are many more miracles concerning my jewelry, but that is enough to let you know that God cares about the things we care about. We just need to ask to receive. God is a lover and a giver.

God Cares for the Little Things

My daughter met her husband in college. He and his family lived in New Jersey.

When our children started getting married, I had heard of so many families getting in big arguments over where the children were going to spend the holidays. I decided that it was not going to happen with our families.

We discussed the situation, and my suggestion was that they take turns going to see their families. One Christmas, they would go to their husband's family, and the next year, they would go to the wife's family. It was talked over with both sides, and it was agreed upon. It has worked wonderfully. When our children all go to their in-laws', my husband and I take off on a vacation for a week. I don't bake and don't do many decorations. We actually look forward to the off years. We enjoy a relaxed time with just the two of us. It is a great time to see the beautiful decorations in different parts of the country, and we are able to see many Christmas programs.

One year, my daughter suggested that we come to New Jersey and spend Christmas with all of them. We loved our son-in-law's family and quickly agreed. We had such a great time and even had tickets to the Follies. What a show—we loved it.

It snowed while we were there, and our son-in-law's father had a snowblower. He and my husband were having such a super grand time in the snow. They were out there for hours. The sun was out, the humidity was very low, and there was no wind. They still talk about the good time they had shoveling and blowing the snow.

While there, we went to a Chinese restaurant. We were able to park right in front of the restaurant. We were having a great time together. We enjoyed the food and the atmosphere. We were there for several hours as people do when they are enjoying themselves.

When we left the restaurant, I went to get into the back of the car. I noticed a gold bracelet on the concrete right beside the car. I said, "Oh my gosh. Somebody lost their gold bracelet." As I picked it up, I said, "Oh my gosh. It's mine!"

Many cars had parked next to us. I believe God blinded their eyes because He knew my husband had purchased it for me. It was one of my favorites. I believe it was called the hugs-and-kisses bracelet.

We think God is only interested in helping us with big things, but I know He cares just as much for the little things in our lives. That was just another one of God's miracles.

Fiftieth-Anniversary Cruise

In 2004, we celebrated our fiftieth wedding anniversary by going on a cruise with our entire family of seventeen. The youngest grandchild was two, and the oldest was eighteen. There were eight adults and nine grandchildren.

We had our plans all set for June 2003. However, we received word from our cruise company in April that the boiler had blown up on our ship. They were going to try to have it repaired by June. We finally had to cancel our trip and didn't go until the next June. We were on the Royal Caribbean ship called *Enchantment of the Sea*.

We lived on Merritt Island and traveled to Fort Lauderdale to board our ship the next day. We spent the night at the Sheraton Yankee Trader Hotel so we would be close to the port. We all had fun playing on the beach that evening, trying to keep the children busy. Some of the children had never been on a cruise ship, and they were very excited. They could hardly wait for the next day to come.

We arrived at the port, got everyone on board, and headed to our rooms. When we entered our room, we said, "Oh my gosh. We are not in the right room. We did not order a room with a balcony." It was a beautiful room. Our kids were right behind us, and they announced that they had upgraded our room to one with a balcony. I couldn't believe how very nice it was of them—and how much we enjoyed that outside balcony. We actually spent quite a bit of time out there, just enjoying the peace and quiet. We felt bad that the others had standard rooms, but we didn't offer to change with any of them. The grandchildren enjoyed the balcony too.

Our first stop was Key West. We rented a good-sized wooden sailboat that came with a captain at the helm. I think they also provided some snacks and drinks. It was so much fun having the boat to ourselves, and we were out there for several hours. The teenage girls thought it was a great time to relax and work on their tans. We went back to the ship for lunch. After that, everyone did their own thing. We had already decided to meet for dinner in the dining room. We went to a show after dinner in the theater.

The next morning, we all met in the dining room for a delicious breakfast and found out we were in Cozumel. The younger children wanted to stay on the ship and attend the children's programs. The rest of us decided to look around Cozumel and do some shopping in the markets. The older girls saw chokers that they liked outside one of the shops. They were two for twenty dollars. My daughter-in-law purchased them.

We then went into a shop further down, and they had the same thing, but it was three for only ten dollars. My daughter-in-law took off down the street to where they had purchased the other chokers. She said, "Hey, you guys took advantage of us. We found them cheaper down the street."

They just ignored her and didn't offer to do anything about it. She decided to stick around their tables, and when someone walked up to look at their merchandise, she would inform them that they could get it cheaper down the street. After this went on for a while, they gave her another choker just to get rid of her. We got a kick out of her boldness, but it worked. After that, we shopped around before we purchased.

After dinner, we all went into the theater for the evening show. The first thing they did was parade the children who had attended their children's programs all around the room. They were all dressed as pirates. It was so cute to see our little ones all dressed up, and they really enjoyed themselves.

The emcee announced that the show was going to be the love and marriage game show. He started searching for people who had been married the least amount of years in the room. I immediately got this funny feeling that he was searching for contestants for the game. I thought, *We will probably be the longest.* I whispered to my husband not to raise his hand.

When the emcee got up to fifty years, our grandchildren and our kids started pointing to us. They were yelling, "Come on, Grampy and Grammy."

The emcee came over to where we were and asked if we had been married fifty years. Actually, it was fifty-one. There were no other couples in the room who had been married as long as we had. Everyone was insisting that we get up and be in the game show as the longest married.

They took us backstage and told us what we were to do. They took the ladies out onto the stage and asked us all the questions first. If you've ever watched the *Newlywed Game,* the questions can get pretty personal—and sometimes a little on the raunchy side for the younger children. That is exactly what happened. It was hard to answer the questions because our grandchildren were sitting out in the audience and listening to every word we were saying. I remember a couple of the questions: What size bra do you wear? Where was the funniest place you ever made out? It was embarrassing to answer those in front of the grandchildren. They brought out the men and asked them the same questions.

The audience really enjoyed our answers, but we were far from the winners. We were both glad that it was over. I think everyone on the ship saw that show, and they would make comments in the elevators and other places when they met up with us. We met many people from being on the show. They even gave us a video of it.

Our next stop was Belize. We split up when we got off the ship because some of them were doing excursions, and we were just interested in looking around. Some went out on a catamaran to a little island and went snorkeling. They all enjoyed that, and the water was so blue and clear. One of our grandsons was walking on the sidewalk, and a young guy came out of a bar and upchucked right in front of him. He didn't think much of that. My daughter-in-law told him that is why you don't drink.

The next day, we were on the ship all day. They had different things going on that you could attend. They had gold day, and I purchased some of that. There was rock climbing, a talent show, and swimming. The kids took part in all or some of that. I talked my husband into going to bingo. He didn't play, but I finally played a game and won seventy-five dollars. He didn't have too much to say about bingo after that. We do not play the lottery and that kind of stuff. There wasn't much going on at that time, and I decided it would be fun to watch bingo.

We arrived back in Fort Lauderdale the next day and then went to Merritt Island. We really enjoyed the trip and made so many memories. The children still talk about that and wish we could go again.

Big Bird

I STOPPED BY MY DEAR friend's house on Merritt Island to pick up something. It was quite a number of years ago. Since I didn't intend to stay long, I left the car running. Being a great friend, I stayed longer than I had planned.

I entered through the front door, but when I left, she told me to go out through the garage, As she opened the garage door, we saw a humongous great white heron. It was taller than us and had a very long beak and round, beady eyes. My friend quickly pushed the button to close the garage door. We looked at each other and then broke out laughing. She suggested that I go out the front door. We got to the front door and saw the same big bird.

She told me the bird had followed her when she was out walking the day before. She quickly made it back to the house and went in to get a glass of water. She came back out on the porch swing to rest and cool off. She thought it had gone on its way, but it showed up again and came toward her. She went inside and watched through the door as he started going down the street. She thought it was safe to go back out on the swing, but it turned around and came back toward her porch. She grabbed some bread from the kitchen and threw it at the bird, but it would have nothing to do with it. She guessed it wanted some sort of fish. She made a decision to stay inside.

After we saw it standing at the front door, we decided to go back to the garage. I would make a run for the car. That crazy bird could read our minds because it came running around the corner and met us as the garage door went up. My friend suggested that she would go back to the front door, and if it came back around to the porch, I could make a run from the garage.

All the time this was happening, we were in stitches. We were laughing at ourselves and how that dumb bird seemed to be in control of the situation. Ha! Finally, that worked. I went out of the garage and dashed to the car. As I drove off, my friend peeked out the front door. The bird was still peeking in at her. It looked so funny, and I couldn't stop laughing.

Inaugural Ball

MY VERY CLOSE FRIEND was involved in politics back in the eighties. She worked on Capitol Hill and was invited to the very distinguished presidential event: the inaugural ball. Everyone who was anyone hoped to receive an invitation.

When the invitation arrived, she felt like Cinderella. She never dreamed she could attend such an event. With excitement, she began shopping for her attire. She looked all over Washington for the perfect dress, but she was on a very tight budget. She came across something that was very appropriate and ladylike. The old-fashioned dress had a lot of lace, a high-necked collar, and a ruffled bottom. When she tried it on, she realized she needed to purchase a waist cincher (corset). It gave her the perfect look, but it was a little snug.

She had to find the perfect shoes. As she looked and looked for what she wanted, she had to settle for a pair of shoes that matched the dress. They happened to be one size too small. *Oh well*, she thought, *that won't be a problem because we'll be sitting at tables*. She wouldn't have to stand except to stand up and breathe now and then. Surprise, surprise, there were no tables and no chairs—not even one.

The night grew long as they anxiously waited for the arrival of Ronald and Nancy Reagan. Two hours later, she knew she had no choice—even if she missed the entrance of Nancy and Ronnie. She frantically began looking for the ladies' room. She needed relief and fast! She prayed there would be an empty stall. She threw open the door, pried off her shoes, and tore open the buttons on her dress to get to the waist cincher. By this time, the pressure and gas were unbearable. She took time to relax, rub her feet, and take a few deep breaths.

She hated to think of having to put herself back together again in that miserable outfit and return to the festivities. It all may have looked good, but it sure didn't feel good. She was asking herself why she had settled for those tight shoes and that miserable, stupid waist cincher to look like she had stepped out of *Gone with the Wind*. She was creating some wind of her own while in the stall, and she was praying the night would end soon. Her concerned husband was waiting patiently outside the ladies' room, hoping everything came out okay and everything got tucked back in so they could return to the festivities.

Finally, Nancy and Ronnie showed up and did the presidential waltz. My friend looked at her husband and said sternly, "We're out of here!"

As they were driving home, she threw off the shoes and the waist cincher. She was sitting in the front seat of the car. Suddenly, a truck pulled up next to where she sat. Her husband frantically hollered, "Cover up. Cover up!"

She replied, "Oh, what the heck. I need relief and fast. He's probably seen it all before."

Thankfully, it was dark when they pulled into their driveway at nine thirty. They had expected a long, enjoyable evening at the ball and not getting home until at least midnight. She made her husband promise to never breathe a word of the disappointing, miserable evening.

When a friend called the next morning to inquire about the big night, my friend said, "Darlin', I had the time of my life. I was gliding across the ballroom floor as I mingled with very important people."

She knew no one would ever know the real truth about how Cinderella almost exploded at the ball and came home way before midnight with no glass slipper.

What a Smart Mom

I DON'T KNOW WHO THIS mother was, but she was about as smart as they come. She had all the right answers to nip this kid's pride in the bud.

❊❊❊

My son Henry came home from school one day with a big smile across his face. "Hey, Mom. We had a substitute teacher in sociology class today. He was super smart, and I found out some really neat stuff. Mom, you won't really want to hear this, but I found out that kids have rights! Did you know there is a bill called the Children's Bill of Rights? I have all kinds of rights I didn't know about. According to him, kids don't have to make our beds, clean our rooms, or allow you to tell us what to think, what words can come out of our mouths, or even what clothes we can wear.

"Listen to this one, Mom. As far as religion goes, I can choose what to believe—and even if and where to go. I'm sorry. You have no right on that one either. My choices are totally up to me. Even praying to the Lord, I don't even have to pray—now or any other day.

"I know tattoos are on your list of things I cannot have, but now I can have them from head to toe, and that will be just fine. And I can pierce whatever and wherever I desire.

"I really like this one, Mom, and you'd better listen carefully. You ever try to touch me with your hand or with a rod, I can have you put in jail by showing them the marks on my rear end. Also, don't ever try to touch me in any other way—no hugs or kisses. That is also child abuse.

"I don't want to hear anything about me having the right morals like your mama taught to you. That's just more control, and that's illegal too. Mom, now that I have all these rights, I can call Children's Services Division, known as CSD."

Whoa. Who is this kid? He can't belong to me. I wanted to kick him out of the house—and as far and as high as I could kick. A thought came to my mind. What a great time to teach him all about the Parents' Bill of Rights! As I thought about it more and more, I could have some fun. I started thinking of all the things I could plan to do with this kid who thinks he has so many rights. A big smile spread across my face. *He's in trouble now. He is messing with a pro.*

The next day, I said, "Hey, Henry. Let's go shopping. We'll have lots of fun." Our first stop was at Goodwill. "Pick out all you want. There's all kinds of clothes and more. Oh, by the way, I called CSD. They said Goodwill, K-Mart, and Walmart would all be just fine with them. They also shared lots of other well-known secondhand stores.

"Are you hungry? I'm hungry too, but I decided we don't have time to stop or even pick up anything. Look in my purse. There may be a pack of stale crackers that will hold you until dinner. Better save your appetite for dinner. I've decided we will be having liver and onions, which is my very favorite. You also need to be thinking about what you are going to take in your sack lunch tomorrow. You will be fixing your own from now on.

"I was checking the calendar this morning and noticed that your driver's test was scheduled for tomorrow. Don't worry.

I cancelled it since the CSD is unconcerned. The parents can decide what is best for their children since they have rights also."

In a very soft voice, he said, "Mom, can we pick up a movie to watch tonight on my VCR?"

I said, "Oh my gosh. I'm very sorry. I forgot to tell you I sold some of your things to another boy. My car tires were really wearing down. I also sold your TV, and besides that, you don't have a room right now. I rented it out to a friend of mine. You will have to sleep on the couch. CSD only requires me to provide a roof over your head.

"I went online and put all your major toys on eBay. The big Jet Ski, your Rollerblades, and your favorite of all: the four-wheeler. And your allowance now goes to me. Won't that be really neat? I can buy some things that I could really use. Your clothing won't be brand names now, and I'll be choosing what we eat. How does this all sound? The Parent's Bill of Rights versus the Children's Bill of Rights?

"Think about this. You may have misunderstood some of what the teacher was telling you. It is always better to obey your parents than it is those who maybe mean right—but it just doesn't come out right. Nothing against teachers, but if they don't have kids yet, there is a lot they have to learn. Hey, big man. What's with all the tears? Why are you on your knees? Maybe you learned really fast. It is better to look to God and obey your mom and dad instead of CSD."

The Osprey Nest

WHEN LIVING ON MERRITT Island in our big house on Honeymoon Lake, we had the pleasure of having an old tree that had broken off about halfway up, leaving only three short stubby branches at the top. The ospreys decided it was the perfect spot to build a nest, lay their eggs, and hatch them. We would be able to watch the whole procedure.

The male osprey would arrive first and start dancing over the nest and making loud calls. We didn't understand what this was all about at first. This went on for quite a few days, and then the female arrived. They were both dancing and making noises. The male did it to show the other birds that it was his territory— and he was advertising for a mate. Both of them would have a courtship on the nest.

It was so much fun to watch them build that nest. The mostly dead tree was perfect for holding the nest securely in place. The male and female took turns getting the branches for the nest. One would make three trips, and then the other would take a turn. They would fly to the edge of a big tree and come out with a good-sized branch in their beaks. They would work and work to get it in the nest and then take off two more times for more branches. The other one would take a turn doing the same thing. It took several weeks to get the nest just the way they wanted it. It appeared to be about three or four feet across. They came back to the same nest every year and would add to it until it was pretty deep. We were able to have the joy of watching them for several years.

At one point, we had a very bad storm. One of the limbs broke off, and most of the nest fell to the ground. They frantically tried building it back, but after they would get so far, part of it would fall to the ground. They finally gave up and moved to another place. We were so disappointed. We always loved watching them prepare for their family. It was hard to get any work done because we didn't want to miss anything. I always said it would have been great for people in a nursing home to be able to watch it all going on.

After they finished the nest and the female laid her eggs, it took thirty to forty days for the eggs to hatch. It was important that the eggs stay warm and protected. If a bird of almost any kind came near, the osprey would chase it away in a very angry way.

To eat, the male osprey would dive into the lake from a pretty high distance and pick up a fairly large fish. He would fly up into a tree and start tearing that fish apart for himself or take it up into the nest to feed the female who was sitting on her eggs. He would sit on the eggs at times and let her dive for her own fish.

After the eggs hatched, they would feed the little ones. If they happened to drop the fish, they did not fly down to pick it up. They started all over, diving for another one in the lake.

Only three or four eggs hatched. The nests were pretty deep, and it was hard to see the babies. When they were older, we could see their little heads bobbing around in the nest. They were fully grown in about seven or eight weeks and started trying to fly. They would perch on the edge of the nest or on a limb and practice flying and then perching. After many days, they would finally follow their parents to look for food and dive for fish.

They never came back because of the broken limb. We hope they built their new nest close to someone else's home so they can have all the fun that we had over the years.

Possum and Family Come to Visit

WHILE IN THE PROCESS of building our home on Merritt Isle, we had a surprise visit from a mother possum and her four small babies.

My mother and I were sitting inside our unfinished living room. We watched the builders working on the stair railings around the upstairs balcony. The house was three stories high and had decks on each floor that overlooked Honeymoon Lake.

The French doors in our living room opened out to the second-floor deck. Our house was on a hill, and the deck was level with the ground in the front. The mother possum walked slowly toward the French doors—followed by her four babies. I jumped up and went to the French doors.

She slowly turned around and started going back the way she came. She would go a little ways, fall over, and stay there for a few seconds. She would get back up, go a little farther, fall over, and get up. When she got to the end of the deck, she went down the hill toward the lake. She continued to fall over and slowly get back up—all the way to the lake. There were some small mangrove bushes that grew along the edge of the lake to prevent the erosion of the banks.

We realized that she was ill and was trying to get her babies where they would have water and protection in the bushes. The next day, we went down to look for her. She was dead at the edge of the water, and her babies were close by. We called the county animal control, and they came to take the babies.

It is interesting how God gives animals the same desire to protect and love their little ones, just as we humans do.

Memories of the Big House

In 1983, WE BUILT and moved into a large home on Honeymoon Lake. Our home was three stories and built on a small hill. We had a full basement, which was very unusual in Florida. The walk-in basement led to the lake.

One half of the basement was a workroom for my husband. His hobby was woodworking, and he built many beautiful pieces of furniture over the years.

The other half was a playroom or a recreation room for the kids and adults. It had a pool table, a ping-pong table, all sorts of games, and a trampoline outside.

Our grandchildren loved that house, and when they would come to visit, they immediately headed for the basement. We wouldn't see much of them until they got hungry or it was mealtime. Many memories were made for them in that house.

Living on a lake, they loved when Grampy took them on adventures. They would all jump in the boat and head for the woods across the lake. They would stay busy for a while looking for horseshoe crab shells or other odd items and come back with all sorts of things to show the parents and Grammy. They loved these adventures.

In the summer, we would have the granddaughters for a week and then the grandsons. We would buy each of the kids a disposable camera, and they could take pictures of anything or everything we had planned for them during the week. We took them to Cocoa Beach, SeaWorld, and Disney. We developed the pictures and purchased scrapbooks for the girls. We planned a day to fill out their scrapbooks, and they could decorate them as they desired. I purchased special sheets of decorations and scraps of lace for them to use. I think they still have those scrapbooks.

We planned different things for the boys during their week. Scrapbooks were not their thing. We gave them choices about what to do. We took them to special places, parks, and the zoo. We had as much fun as they did. We looked forward to those times as much as they did, although it took a lot of planning and money on our part!

One year at Christmas, all the children and grandchildren were visiting. In central Florida, it was unusual to get freezing weather on the coast. That year, we ended up having several days of below-freezing weather. The city could not power everyone at the same time and had to cycle the electricity every few hours. As the hostess of a large crowd, I was wondering what we were going to do about the food. We had to get creative. We were able to cook the turkey on the charcoal grill, and for the small amount of time the electricity would be on, we would microwave the side dishes. We ended up having a great time. We had a delicious meal, a great time opening gifts, and played so many fun games. We had two fireplaces, which helped keep us warm. Our one grandchild at the time was just a baby, but we were able to keep her warm and content with a full tummy.

During this time together, we realized the important things in life are not having all the conveniences of our modern world. It was about the time together, working together, and coming up with ideas for how to get through that time. It made us think how the early settlers had to live, and it made us more appreciative of how much easier we had it than they did.

The memories we made that day are still very vivid to all of us. The Lord knew it would draw us closer, and He was there with us all through the experience.

The house was too much work when we got older. It was hard, but we decided to put it up for sale. I asked my daughter-in-law to have their children pray the house would sell. She said, "Mom, they are not going to pray that the house sells. They love that house."

I am not sure if they did any praying since it took a year to sell the house. The children and grandchildren still talk about the big house and all the memories associated with it.

Burning Tablecloth

My sister-in-law embroidered a beautiful Christmas tablecloth. She worked on it for many months. We all knew how much hard work had gone into it. It was a lovely piece of work and something to be proud of.

It was my brother's turn to have Christmas for the family at his home. His wife had just finished the tablecloth and was anxious to show everyone her beautiful creation. The table did look especially pretty with the greenery, candles, and an arrangement in the center.

After we finished dinner and had cleaned up the dishes, everything was pretty much back in order. We all went out to their pool. It was a beautiful day, and we were having fun as most families do. We were laughing, joking, and having a good time together.

Our son-in-law had gone to sleep on the couch by the table. After a short nap, he smelled smoke. Oh no! We had forgotten to blow out the candles, and they had set some of the greenery on fire. That caused the tablecloth to catch on fire. He yelled, "Fire, fire!"

That caught our attention really quickly.

Another son-in-law grabbed the tablecloth and jumped into the ice-cold swimming pool with no concern for his clothing or shoes. His intentions were great. He thought he could save the tablecloth. He kept trying to push the tablecloth under the water, but it kept floating. The burning continued, and it was too late. It was so heartbreaking for all of us, but we felt especially sorry for our sister-in-law to see her work of art destroyed. Thinking of all the time and effort she had put into it, she decided she couldn't see her way to ever do another one. Her eyes had been failing, and she had been diagnosed with macular degeneration.

We were so thankful that God woke up our son-in-law in time to save more than just the tablecloth. It could have been much worse than just losing a tablecloth.

Moving to Jacksonville

AFTER MAKING THE HUGE decision to sell our home and move to Jacksonville, we had a large house sale. After downsizing to a much smaller home, we had to part with many pieces of our furniture and other items we didn't have room for.

What we decided to keep, we had to put in storage on Merritt Island. We were planning to rent a small apartment until our home was finished, but our son-in-law wouldn't have it any other way. We went to live with them until our house was finished.

We took their office and brought only what we needed to Jacksonville. This included our bed, vanity, TV, chair, bedside table, lamp, and a file cabinet for our business papers. It was crowded, but it worked fine. We had no idea it would take so long for our house. It took a total of nine months. We said we had to birth our new home.

It was a joy to be able to spend time with them and their two children. Our grandson was three years old, and our granddaughter was one year old. They now have four children. We never had any disagreements or problems. We would try to spend our evenings in our room to give them space. However, the two little ones were usually in our room until bedtime. Of course, we enjoyed every minute of it.

When the time came to move into our house, we had to rent a large U-Haul truck to get everything in it. We had other vehicles for the smaller things. We had a beautiful grand piano that we were most concerned about. We carefully covered it with padding of all sorts. We tried strapping it to the side of the truck so it wouldn't move around and get scratched.

We finally got on our way to Jacksonville and were hardly out of Merritt Island when the truck broke down. Can you imagine the scare and concern that came over us? What would U-Haul do about it? We didn't want to unpack everything and start over. We called them, and they said they would have a tow truck pull us to Jacksonville, which was two hours away.

After several hours in the heat, the tow truck showed up. When he got the U-Haul ready to tow, it was tilted because the front of the U-Haul had to be considerably off the ground. Oh no. What about our piano? Would everything slide toward the rear of the truck?

As we were following in a car behind him, much to our dismay, we viewed the truck bouncing up the road in excess of seventy miles an hour. Can you imagine the beating everything in the U-Haul was taking? We had been so careful in how we packed everything, and then that happened.

We didn't get to Jacksonville until late and couldn't unload until the next day. I was so anxious about what we would find when we finally were able to lift the door of the U-Haul.

The next morning, we all held our breath as the door went up. As we had feared, the piano had taken a rough ride. It had come loose from the side of the truck where we thought it had been secured with adequate cushions. We finally decided not to worry about it. We would just have it refinished. Several other things were slightly damaged, but we were able to repair them. We were happy it wasn't any worse.

Our daughter and her family were probably happy that we were finally moving out after nine months of sharing their home. It was a real blessing for us to have the opportunity to spend time with them and enjoy the children.

We are very happy in our new home. I love to decorate, and it gave me many walls and rooms to work on. We know that God had His hand in our moving to Jacksonville. We have met many wonderful people and found a great church.

Smart Dad

THANKSGIVING WAS ONLY A few days away, and the kids hadn't made it home for several years. The father knew how much he and their mother would like them to be with them this year. He did some deep thinking about it.

After much thinking, he called his son. He said, "Kevin, I hate to call and bring you this bad news, but I've been putting this off for some time. I just can't put up with it anymore. Your mother and I are going to call it quits. We just can't stand each other anymore. We are at each other with every word. We are having a miserable marriage. We both have had all we can take with each other. We're even sleeping in different bedrooms. Your sister needs to know this also. Why don't you call her?"

Kevin never thought he would hear his father talk that way. They had always had a perfect marriage. The son was at a loss for words, but he couldn't wait to tell his sister and see what she had to say. After telling her what their dad shared, Karen shouted, "Have they gone crazy? They will absolutely not quit their marriage. They will never get a divorce. Don't worry. I'll take care of it. We've got to bring them back to their senses."

Karen quickly called her dad. She shouted at him and had a few choice words for him. She told him not to do anything until she got there. Her brother would also be there tomorrow. "Are you listening to me, Dad? Don't do anything! Don't make any moves in that direction."

Dad hurriedly went to his wife and said, "I found a way to get the kids here for Thanksgiving—and they are going to pay their own ways. They will be here tomorrow."

Flooded with Water

RIGHT AFTER WE MOVED into our new home in Jacksonville and worked so hard getting everything just the way we wanted it, we had a big surprise. My husband, my son, and our son-in-law had just finished laying the hardwood floors, which was a lot of very hard work. They looked beautiful, and we were all so proud of their work.

Before I left to go somewhere the next week, I washed a load of clothes. I had done it quite early and assumed they were finished washing.

I had left around ten o'clock and was on my way home about five. My cell phone rang, and my husband shouted, "Where are you? The house is flooded."

My heart jumped in my throat. Oh, Lord. We had just finished decorating. I told my husband that I would be there soon.

When he got home from work, he saw water coming out from under the garage door. He wondered where it could be coming from. He found out the washer had somehow malfunctioned, and the water had run all over the laundry room, the kitchen, a small portion of the family room, and a small area in the living room. It had run out into the garage, under the baseboards, and into the bedroom closets. Our big concern was the hardwood floors and what it would do to them.

By the time I arrived home, my husband had the Shop-Vac slurping up the water. He had pulled back the carpet from the walls. He had our dehumidifier going, and almost every towel we owned was on the floors, trying to absorb the moisture from penetrating into the wood.

We were hoping and praying that the floors could be saved, but by the next day, they were buckling up. We were tripping as we tried to walk on them. We knew they all had to be replaced. It was like starting over again. All the furniture had to be moved so the floors could be replaced. My husband said it was too soon for him and the guys to do the job again. His knees were still feeling the pain from the first time.

The first contractor we hired worked for one day and didn't show up again. His excuse was that his grandmother had died and he had to go to the funeral. That was the last we ever heard from him. We searched for another contractor, and within a few days, the job was finished. We started putting all the furniture back into its place.

My dear sweet husband was able to do all the cleanup from the water spill, removing all the wood flooring and baseboards, and doing all the preparation for the new flooring, which also included a vapor barrier over the concrete floor. Fortunately, our homeowner's insurance covered the complete project, including the work my husband did. After paying for the wood and the installer, we had enough money left to screen in our lanai.

It turned out that what seemed to be a tragedy and a financial burden, God turned it into a blessing. We have enjoyed the lanai, and it makes a great place for entertaining family and friends.

A Granddaughter

WHEN MY DAUGHTER WAS pregnant with her third child, I always enjoyed going with her to see the ultrasound. It was so exciting to see what miracle the Lord was creating. I always enjoyed when that little one came popping out and was able to go from breathing living in the water or fluid to instantly breathing the air the good Lord provides for all of us to survive.

When it was her turn to be called back to have the ultrasound done, we jumped up to see if it was going to be a girl or a boy. They already had a boy and a girl and didn't really care what this one was going to be.

The nurse came in and prepared my daughter for the ultrasound. I remember going with my daughter to see the other two children's ultrasound. When the nurse was looking at the pictures, she would be awing and oohing over what she could see. "There's its little hand. Can you see the little nose? Oh, yes, it is a boy."

When the nurse was looking at this picture, it was complete silence. I kept thinking, *Isn't she going to tell us what she is seeing?* After some time, she said, "I'll be right back." I immediately thought, *Oh dear. This doesn't seem right.* She came back with the doctor, and he looked and looked without uttering a word. Finally, he said, "It looks like a little girl. It does look like one leg is shorter than the other."

It hit us both like a knife going into our hearts.

My daughter said, "Did I do it, Doctor?"

He assured her immediately that it was nothing she had caused. "I don't really know why these things sometimes happen."

We asked if there was any chance it would continue to grow in the last few months. His answer didn't encourage us.

We had been praying for a healthy baby, but now we were asking everyone to ask God to help that little leg to grow. When the time came for her to be born, it all went well, but she was born with a short leg below the knee.

They found a local doctor who was familiar with it, but he suggested that they go to a doctor in Baltimore, Maryland, who specialized in correcting the problem. She has had several surgeries and treatments of stretching the leg. She keeps growing, so they have to continue with the stretching. She will have hip surgery at the age of eleven and possibly hip replacement at the age of twenty.

This has not slowed her down. She runs, maybe not quite as fast as others, took tennis lessons and dance lessons, and can do almost anything else any child can do. She is a beautiful girl with a sweet spirit and personality. The Lord has also blessed her with a beautiful voice. She enjoys acting and keeps the family laughing with her comical remarks and actions.

Her family and friends have all been blessed by her life. We know God has a special purpose for her and that she was born this way for a reason. She has been a tough little girl during all the surgeries, and she never complains. She is a special girl who we all love and care for. Like her younger sister wrote on a large birthday card: "I love you just the way the Lord made you!"

Eleven Leadership Traits

My Husband Shared With me that, on June 26, 1999, in the wee hours of the morning, a series of thoughts began to run through his mind over and over again. He finally couldn't sleep and got up three different times to write down the thoughts that kept coming to him.

In the morning, when he went to his desk, this is what he had written:

Leadership Traits by Frank Howald

- vision of an inventor
- purpose of an explorer
- strategy of a general
- zeal of a missionary
- thrill of the hunt
- confidence of a champion
- tenacity of a termite
- endurance of a marathon runner
- excited as a young lover
- loving like a mother
- purity of refined gold

Confirmation of the source came when he read his Bible devotions for the day in Psalm 16:7. "I will bless the Lord who has given me counsel; My heart also instructs me in the night seasons."

Our Grandson's Senior Moment

ONE TRADITION AT MY son's house on Thanksgiving is to watch the parade and then the dog show. Their oldest son was a senior in high school, so Thanksgiving 2009 was no different.

The extended family was converging on their house for dinner. Our daughter-in-law was trying to concentrate on all the food preparation. However, right in the middle of it, she decided she should change her clothes before everyone arrived. She dashed upstairs with her oldest daughter following her.

After they finished upstairs and came back down, her daughter noticed that Lily, her miniature pinscher, was missing. They checked all around the house, in the closets and bathrooms, and then started outside. They yelled out the backyard, and our son took the car to see if he was somewhere in the neighborhood. Her daughter walked down the street and was calling for Lily. She came back in tears because Lily was nowhere to be found.

During this whole time, their oldest son was watching the dog show. He seemed to be oblivious to what was going on in the household. He finally realized that something was amiss. How could he have not noticed all the commotion around the house?

My daughter-in-law asked her son to say a prayer that they could find Lily. He prayed a short prayer, asking the Lord to help them find her. Just as he finished praying, he looked up with a thoughtful look on his face. "I may know where Lily is."

He dashed to the garage and opened the car door. Lily was curled up, fast asleep. He remembered that he had to go to the garage to get something and had Lily in his arms. He couldn't carry the object and Lily, and he put her in the car for safekeeping for the time being. He forgot poor Lily. He came back in the house, triumphantly reunited with Lily. She was fine and didn't know she had been lost. His sister was still in tears, but they were now tears of joy.

They thought of his prayer and said, "Wow, you were the answer to your own prayer!"

An aunt was standing close by and said, "He must have had a *senior* moment."

Lake House Incident

MY SON OWNS A lake house in Starke, Florida, which is a little over an hour from our home. We spent many special holidays, birthdays, and other times relaxing at his house.

It happened to be Father's Day, and we were all gathered to celebrate. We were enjoying ourselves on the dock and watching the kids swimming and taking turns riding the wave runner.

My husband decided he would take a turn, and the grandchildren started yelling, "Come on, Grammy. Ride with Grampy." Water is not one of my favorites. We had both been on the wave runner before, and I just wanted to relax and enjoy the day. However, to finally please them all, I gave in reluctantly and climbed aboard.

At that time, we were looking at different swings for my husband to build. Just about three houses down from our dock, I spotted a swing on the people's porch. I shared it with Frank, and he decided to turn around and go back to get a closer look. He slowly started to turn the wave runner, and I yelled, "Frank, we are going to tip over." And that is exactly what we did. We both flipped over, and the wave runner was upside down. Fortunately, we each had on a life jacket.

Apparently, it must happen to a wave runner quite often. On the bottom, there were directions for how to turn it upright. We had no problem with that. The problem turned out to be getting us back on the wave runner without tipping over again.

161

Somebody had forgotten to tell us there was a step you could pull down to get back on it. Frank would get me up, and he would try to get on—and we would go over again. After about three times, I told him I just couldn't do it anymore. My chest was really hurting with heaviness. We were very close to the shore and a dock. We decided that would be our best bet. About that time, we looked up and our sixteen-year-old grandson was swimming to save us. I called him my hero!

He took us one at a time over to the dock where we could both get on, and then he pulled us back to my son's dock. I couldn't wait to get off since my chest was really hurting. I sat down and asked them to get me some aspirin. I had always heard you should take an aspirin if you think you are having a heart attack. I did that, but it didn't seem to help the pain. I also have a hiatal hernia that acts just like you are having a heart attack, and that is what I believed was going on at that time.

I sat on the deck. Everyone was staring at me and asking if I was all right. Finally, they walked me up to the house, and I got into dry clothes. I just sat there, thinking the pain would let up.

My daughter-in-law had to go back to the church that morning because she had to do something with the youth. When she arrived back, she could see that something was wrong. My hair was wet, and she knows I do not like to get my hair wet. She was concerned about what had happened.

I finally told Frank I wanted to go home. They immediately helped Frank gather our belongings, and we took off. Frank told me that he was taking me to the hospital. It took us a little over an hour to get to the hospital. They took me right in.

The many tests showed that I did have a heart attack. I kept telling them it was probably my hiatal hernia. They said, "Honey, you had a heart attack. Your enzymes were very high."

I was told that there was no damage to my heart, and that was very good news.

I have been fine ever since that incident, but I have not been back on the wave runner. Nobody even asks me if I want to take a ride. Yeah!

Feeling Guilty

WE WENT ON A trip with friends from Merritt Island a few years ago. Our husbands told us we must be sisters because we are so much alike in our likes and dislikes.

One of our likes is shopping. We were able to ditch our husbands for a while and go shopping. We were having a ball in the little shops and with all the goodies. We both love jewelry and found many shops that carried many lovely pieces. We would pick up a bracelet, try it on, show each other, take it off, and grab another. This happened in store after store. Our husbands told us not to be gone too long since we had plans to do something else. We were racing from one store to another. We wanted to hit as many as we could. Since we were leaving the next day, there would be no more time to shop.

We finally decided we better get back or our hubbies would be having a hissy fit.

When I was removing my clothing to get ready for bed, I took off my long-sleeved blouse, and there—shining as bright as could be—was one of the bracelets. It had gotten up high enough on my wrist that I didn't notice it. It was a very light and narrow bracelet with little glass crystals (not diamonds) in it. It was not an expensive one. It was just costume jewelry, but I panicked! The stores were closed and would be closed when we left the next morning. I had no idea what store it came from because we

165

weren't paying attention to the names. We had not purchased anything and had no receipts with names or phone numbers.

I ran next door to my friend's hotel room and shared the story with her.

She said, "Well, we both know you didn't do it on purpose. Just keep it and wear it. There is really nothing you can do about it now." She agreed that it was probably around twenty-five dollars if that much. I felt so badly. I had taken something that I didn't pay for. What was God thinking about it?

That bracelet is one of my favorites now. When I put it on, I think about what happened. It has taught me to be more careful and respectful of other people's property.

I sometimes think God was probably getting a chuckle out of that situation. He knew it was taken by mistake, and He knew me well enough to know that I wouldn't have taken it on purpose. I have to laugh because it is one of my favorites.

God knows how much I love jewelry, and since I wasn't buying any that day, I guess He thought I should have that one. Ha!

Highway 23 All the Way to Ohio

My Husband Grew Up on a farm on Highway 23 in central Ohio. After moving to Florida, he noticed that US 23 started in Jacksonville. He told me that he would like to take US 23 all the way back to Norton, Ohio, where he grew up. That was where we farmed for two years before he was drafted into the army. He thought it would be fun to drive through the countryside and the small towns. It wouldn't be as boring as driving on the interstate.

A few years later, we received word that my oldest sister in Ohio had passed away. Since the funeral wouldn't be for several days, we thought about my husband's desire to take a trip on US 23. We decided it would be the perfect opportunity to take it all the way to Ohio.

Everything went well on our trip until we came to Norton, Virginia. We were waiting for a red light to turn green. We started turning, and the van we were driving just decided to die. We were on the right side of the road as we turned, but we were still right in the way of the rush hour traffic.

We immediately grabbed our phones to call AAA, but our phones were showing no service. We noticed a flea market and fruit stand across the street. My husband decided to go over and see if we could use someone's phone to call for help. However, since it was past five, everything was closed. He came back to the car, and we hoped a police car would soon happen by.

As he stood near the van, a car pulled up and asked if he needed help. He told them the story, jumped in the car with them, and took off. I wondered what he was doing. He didn't even bother to tell me where he was going. I was pretty put out at him. These people could see we were from out of town, and it would be a good opportunity to rob him. Of course, all kinds of things were running through my mind. For some time, I was wondering what I should do. I finally decided I was going to get out of the car. As soon as I did, a small truck pulled up. Two young boys asked if I needed help. I proceeded to tell them our story. They had to go do something but would be back to help me.

They drove off, and another car pulled up. They asked the same thing. I went through my story again, and they told me the car had probably taken my husband about half a mile down the road to an auto supply store. I felt better hearing that, and they asked me if they could take me there. *Am I going to do the same dumb thing my husband did? If I get in a car with strangers, who knows what could happen to me?* I finally decided to go with them. They took me down the road to the auto supply store. They told me they would wait to see what my husband wanted me to do.

I found my husband at a desk. He had called AAA, and they were going to call him back to let him know how soon the truck would be coming. The employees were busy waiting on people, and my husband took it upon himself to answer their phone. This way, he wouldn't miss his call. Can you believe it?

He looked up and said, "What are you doing here? How did you get here?"

I said, "The same way you got here. I took a chance on strangers to bring me here." I let him know that I was pretty put out at him for not letting me know where he was going.

He told me I needed to go back to the car to wait for the tow truck.

I went outside, and my ride was still waiting to take me back to our van. As I got out of their car, I let them know how much I appreciated their help. I stood next to our van. Almost immediately, a car pulled up and asked if I needed help.

I told my story, and the lady said, "I'm going to stay here with you until either your husband, the police, or AAA comes." She pulled over in front of our van and got out. As we were talking, another car pulled up and asked if I needed help. I repeated my story, and they pulled over in front of the first lady's car. They stayed with me too.

Another car pulled over and stayed with me. Next, the police showed up and parked behind me. This made five cars lined up just around the corner from the stoplight. The traffic was all going slowly around us. We were all having a good time chatting. We finally noticed my husband walking toward us.

As he got closer, the tow truck pulled up. I told the people waiting with me that they should go on. I knew they had things to do and places to go, but I appreciated their interest in making sure I was safe and taken care of. I was amazed at how this small country town was so interested in helping strangers.

After loading the van on his truck, we jumped in with the driver. He said, "Where do you want to take it?"

My husband said, "If it were yours, where would you take it?"

He shared a place that he trusted and my husband said, "That sounds great."

We asked him if there was a nice motel around.

He recommended one, drove us several miles to it, and helped unload our luggage and belongings. He made sure they had a room for us. He took my husband and the van all the way back past where he picked us up—plus another mile to the garage. He unloaded the van and left the keys in a lockbox with a note with my husband's name and the motel's phone number. He had to take my husband back to the motel.

He was such a helpful and giving man. Since it was Wednesday night, they had to call him out of a prayer meeting at the church to come help us.

The next morning my husband called the garage and told the owner how the engine had stopped while we were on our way to my sister's funeral in Ohio.

The owner told my husband he would call him when he had figured out the problem. He also said he would loan us his truck. A driver would bring it to us for transportation while he worked on the van, and we could go get breakfast. We took the driver back to the garage and went to eat. We noticed money in the ashtray. I thought, *This man really does trust us with his truck—and now money is staring us in the face.* We made sure nothing happened to that money.

He called my husband and told him the problem was the timing belt. However, his six-bay garage was full, and he wasn't sure how soon he would have an empty bay. We found out later that he emptied the bay of his key mechanic to replace the timing belt in our engine. We're sure he did that because he knew we were anxious to get back on the road to make it to my sister's funeral.

We went back to the motel in his truck and called our family to tell them what had happened. We would be there, but we were not sure when since we had the car trouble.

It could even be an extra day.

We waited patiently, and to our surprise, he called at two thirty to tell us it was ready. They were test-driving it and would have it ready to go by the time we got there.

We quickly loaded up our luggage and other items and checked out of the motel. On the way to the garage, my husband mentioned that it might be quite expensive since we were not the local folks. Several months earlier, we had a similar problem with another vehicle back home—and it cost nearly a thousand dollars.

We arrived at the garage, and my husband asked the owner how much he owed.

He said, "Just go into the office, and my secretary will give you the bill."

When my husband looked at the bill, he couldn't believe the price. He wasn't sure he was reading it correctly. The total for labor and materials was only $540. What a surprise—and what a blessing.

Two weeks later, the owner called us at home and wanted to know how the van was running. It was just another example of the caring, friendly, and loving people of Norton, Virginia.

We thought about the tow truck driver and what a generous man he had been to us. He drove us all over in his truck and was so interested in taking care of all our needs. We agreed that we needed to send him a little gift of love. We sent him a check and a card to thank him again for being so kind to us.

We thought it was quite interesting that all this happened in a small town called Norton, Virginia, since my husband grew up in a small country town called Norton, Ohio.

The trip started out because of a sad event—losing my sister who meant so much to me—and even though we had car trouble, God allowed it to happen in a place where we received so many blessings from His people. It made the journey to Ohio so much more pleasurable.

Woman Has the Last Word

Juﾍﾈ LIVED ON A small lake and decided to take the boat out. It would be a great place to relax and catch up on her letter writing.

She had just gotten all comfy in her boat and was ready to start her first letter when she realized somebody had pulled up next to her.

She looked up, and a man said, "Good morning, ma'am. I'm the game warden in this area. What are you doing out here?"

Odd question. He can see that I am writing. She replied, "Writing a letter."

"I'm sorry, but you can't fish in this area. It is a restricted area."

"But, sir, I just told you I'm writing."

"Yes, but I see you have all the equipment with you. You could start at any moment. I'll have to arrest you and take you in."

She said, "If you do that, I'll have to charge you with sexual assault."

"But I haven't even touched you," the game warden said.

She replied, "That's true, but you have all the equipment. For all I know, you could start at any minute."

My Embarrassing Mistake

My husband and I had to make a trip to Ohio for a death in my husband's family.

My dear niece offered for us to stay with them in their beautiful home. We really enjoyed the time we were able to spend with them, but we were spending most of our time with his family.

We went back to their home one evening after dark, and when we got there, their two grandchildren were visiting. After talking to them for a little bit, my husband got a good look at me and said, "What in the world do you have on your lips?"

I knew immediately what I had done. In the car—in the dark—I had reached in my purse for my lip liner and lipstick before getting back to my niece's home. In the process, I had picked out my eyeliner rather than my lip liner. It is a teal green, which made me look rather strange. I thought they were all looking at me little strange, but I didn't know why until my husband got a good look at my face. I asked my niece why she hadn't said something, and she said she thought I might be trying something new.

It was quite embarrassing, but we have had many laughs about putting my green eyeliner on my lips. I now look twice before I apply my lip liner.

Always Winners

WE HAVE A GRANDSON-IN-LAW who is in real estate. He had an open house at one of his homes, and our son asked if we wanted to go support him. He suggested going out for dinner after the open house. It sounded good to us, and we said, "Sure. It sounds like fun."

When we arrived, it didn't look like he needed our little support. There were cars everywhere and a good-sized white tent with all kinds of snacks and goodies. When we entered the house, a lady asked us to fill out tickets for a drawing. I asked if our husbands could also sign up and mentioned that we always win. She laughed and said that was great.

We toured the lovely home, and they announced it was time to go out to the tent for the drawing. Everyone gathered under the tent and started nibbling on the goodies. My husband and I were chatting with someone when we heard my husband's name called. We looked at each other to be sure we both heard it, and people started calling out to us. "You won. You won!"

We said, "Well, what did we win?" We hadn't even asked what the drawing was for. It was a sixty-five-inch Vizio TV. They also gave us a gift bag with a hundred-dollar gift card for Firehouse Subs and a Publix gift card for one hundred dollars. We told the lady we always won—and we did.

We had an area above our fireplace for the TV, but we needed a fifty-five-inch TV instead of the sixty-five-inch one. I remembered the bank that had donated it and had even talked to the representative who was there. He had even given us his card.

After we got the TV home, we measured to be sure. We needed the fifty-five-inch one. It had been purchased from Costco. I called them, and they said they would be glad to exchange it for the fifty-five-inch one, but they needed the member's number who purchased it in order to do that. I hated to call him and ask for his Costco membership number, but I didn't really have a choice. I called him, and he immediately said, "Let me get you that number." I thanked him again, and we took off for Costco. They quickly exchanged it. We brought it home, and it worked beautifully. We had just talked about getting a new high-definition TV, and the good Lord supplied it. We gave our old TV to our daughter's family, and they are still enjoying it.

I told them we always won because we had been fortunate in being blessed at other gift drawings.

Make Up Your Mind

A POLICE OFFICER STOPPED MARILEE, a blonde, for speeding and asked her very nicely if he could see her license.

In a huff, she replied, "I wish you guys would make up your mind. Just yesterday, you take away my license—and then today, you expect me to show it to you."

Two Things Wrong

A GORGEOUS YOUNG REDHEAD, SAGE, went to the doctor and said that her she didn't understand why her body hurt wherever she touched it.

"That doesn't seem normal," the doctor said. "Show me."

She pushed on her left arm and screamed. She pushed her back and screamed even more. She pushed her knee and screamed. Everywhere she touched, she screamed.

The doctor said, "You're not a natural redhead, are you?"

"Well, no," she said. "I'm actually a blonde."

"I thought so," the doctor said. "Your finger is broken."

Which Is It?

RICH, A HIGHWAY PATROLMAN, pulled alongside a speeding car on the freeway. Glancing at the car, he couldn't believe that the blonde behind the wheel was crocheting. Realizing that she was oblivious to his flashing lights and siren, the trooper cranked down his window, turned on the bullhorn, and yelled, "Pull over!"

"No," the blonde yelled back. "It's a scarf!"

Who's First?

AN AMERICAN, A RUSSIAN, and a blonde were talking one day.

The American said, "We were the first on the moon."

The Russian said, "We were the first in space."

The blonde said, "So what? We're going to be the first on the sun!"

The other two looked at each other and shook their heads.

The Russian said, "You can't land on the sun, you idiot! You'll burn up!"

The blonde replied, "We're not stupid, you know. We're going at night."

Repeat Act

A PRIEST WAS DRIVING DOWN to New Jersey and was stopped for speeding in New York.

The trooper smelled alcohol on the priest's breath and saw an empty wine bottle on the floor of the car. "Father, have you been drinking?"

"Just water," the priest said.

"Then why do I smell wine?" the trooper said.

The priest picked up the bottle, took a taste, and said, "Good Lord! He's done it again."

Worth the Cost

GRANDMA AND GRANDPA WERE visiting their son. Grandpa was looking for some aspirin in the son's medicine cabinet and saw a bottle of Viagra. He asked the son if he could have one.

The son said, "I don't think you should take one, Dad. They're very strong and very expensive."

"Tell me how much," Grandpa said.

The son said, "Grandpa, they are fourteen dollars."

"Let me have one. I have been wanting to try one, and before we leave in the morning, I'll put the money under the pillow."

The next morning, the son found $114 under the pillow. He called Grandpa and said, "I told you each pill was fourteen dollars—not a hundred and fourteen."

"I know," Grandpa said, "but Grandma threw in the extra hundred."

Who Was She?

SANDRA, A FIFTY-YEAR-OLD, HAD a heart attack. While she was on the operating table, she had a near-death experience. She asked God, "Am I going to die?"

God said, "No, you have another thirty-five years, six months, and five days to live."

After Sandra was feeling better, she decided to continue her stay in the hospital and have a total makeover. She had a facelift, liposuction, and a tummy tuck. She also changed her hair color. Since she had so much more time to live, she thought she would make the most of it.

When the time came to leave the hospital, she was so excited about the new life ahead of her that she wasn't paying attention to what she was doing. As she was crossing the street, she was killed by a truck.

Standing before God, she said, "I thought you said I had another thirty-five years, six months, and five days to live. Why did you allow me to get hit by that big truck?"

God answered, "Well, I didn't recognize you as anyone I created!"

Our Precious Chloe

A YEAR AGO, I DECIDED it would be nice to have a dog. My husband finally agreed, and we knew there was a lady in our subdivision who was connected to an organization called Anna's Angels. The group mainly took in rescued Shih Tzus. I contacted her, and she told me they had just received a fifteen-pound black and white female Shih Tzu.

If we were interested, we could go to a veterinarian to see the dog. They had cleaned her up and given her the necessary shots for a dog her size and age. When she went in, she was covered with fleas and looked like she had been on her own for quite a while. They had picked her up in a small town not too far away. She looked like she had already had puppies. They thought she had been used for breeding purposes and had possibly got loose and run away.

We immediately rushed to take a look at her, and as they brought her out, she was all cleaned up. The fleas had been taken care of, and we knew that she was meant for us. I took her outside for a little walk, and she proved that she was housebroken, which rated high on my scale. They suggested that we take her home for a few days to see if she was suitable for our home. The doctor guessed that she was around one or two years old.

On the way home, we stopped at a pet store to purchase a leash, food, treats, and a dog dish. Sounds like we had already made up our mind to keep her, right?

She seemed to accept our home as her home right away, and there was no question in our minds either—she was part of our family.

We took her in a few weeks later to have her spayed. That doctor guessed that she was no more than three years old. We decided we would count her as a two-year-old. We have had her for a year and now we say she is three years old.

We decided to purchase a cage to put her in when we left the house. Well, that was a waste of money. She did not take to that cage at all. She would literally tear it apart.

The pad we purchased to put in the bottom of the cage would be in shreds after she clawed it to pieces. The water bottle would be broken, and no matter what we tried, she was not going to accept it. We finally tried leaving her free in the house, not knowing what we would find when we returned. Thankfully, she hadn't caused any harm.

After we first got her, my husband was working in the yard. I decided to put one of the dining room chairs in front of the windows and put Chloe in the chair so she could watch him work.

From then on, whenever we had to leave, she would jump up on the chair. She stays in that chair until we return. It may be one hour or six or more hours. She is always watching for our return. She is always anxious to see us, and the first thing she does after greeting us is run to her water dish. We know she has been in that chair the entire time we are gone. If either of us leaves the house, she will sit in that chair and watch until we return.

She has been a real blessing to us. One of the best things about her is that she is not a barker. I dislike a dog that barks at everything and won't stop. She only barks once when she needs to go outside, and we know we better move fast because she means business.

We have become very close buddies. She will only go outside for a walk if one of us is right behind her. She will not even let the grandchildren take her. When we are sitting on the couches, she is either down at my feet or over at the other couch at the feet of my husband. If our feet are on the floor, she rests her face on them.

When we take her for a walk, she loves the small dogs. She doesn't want to leave them after all the sniffing of each other. If she sees large dogs coming, she turns in the other direction and doesn't want to have anything to do with them.

Many people in the neighborhood know Chloe and always have to stop to pet her and make a fuss over her. One man even offered my husband five hundred dollars for her.

We know that God had her picked especially for us and knew exactly what we needed. She exceeds all of our expectations. She is very calm and doesn't get all excited except when we come home. We have a wonderful neighbor who Chloe adores. She keeps her when we go on vacation, and they get along fabulously.

My husband came in from working outside recently and needed to take a rest. He was too dirty for the couch and caught a few winks on the floor. Chloe flopped over on her back—just like my husband—and had her head right next to my husband's shoulder. It was so cute. I grabbed the camera and took a picture. Many people have really enjoyed that picture. My husband rates right at the top with Chloe, and she insists on being inside or outside or wherever he happens to be.

Diamond the Dog

THREE YEARS AGO, SARAH and Tom were fortunate enough to adopt an amazing dog. Diamond had some habits that weren't so good. She loved to investigate their visitor's luggage to see if there was anything she would like to add to her collection of toys in the basement. They always warned the guests, but they would often forget and come up with missing objects. They would always find them among her other treasures in the toy box in the basement, and she was very particular that her toys stay in the toy box.

Sarah was diagnosed with breast cancer and scheduled a double mastectomy. She was sure the outcome was not going to be good. She had a feeling she was going to die.

The night before the surgery, she thought about what was going to happen to Diamond. Three-year-old Diamond liked Tom, but he was her dog. Sarah was very sad. She called Diamond, and they cuddled on the couch until it was time to go to bed.

The surgery was even harder than she thought it would be. She was in the hospital for more than two weeks. The doctor finally told her he thought she was strong enough to go home. When she arrived home, she was exhausted. Tom made her a bed on the couch because she was too weak to make it up the steps to their bedroom. She immediately was fast asleep. Diamond stayed close and kept an eye out for her.

When Sarah awoke, she called Diamond, but he wouldn't come. She wondered why, but she fell asleep. When Sarah woke up, she knew something was wrong. She could hardly move. Her head and body felt heavy and hot. The panic soon turned into laughter when Sarah realized the problem. She was literally covered with every treasure Diamond owned! While she was sleeping, Diamond had made trip after trip to the basement. He brought his favorite loving mistress all his favorite things in life. That's what you call blanketed with love.

It wasn't long before Sarah was up and about. She completely forgot about dying. She and Diamond began living again. They would go for long walks, going farther and farther every day. Diamond is still a character. He steals treasures and stashes them in his toy box, but Sarah remains his greatest treasure. She has been free of cancer for more than fifteen years.

It is interesting how animals are so sensitive to how we feel, especially if we are ill. They take on a sad, droopy expression. They whine and are miserable too. They know something is not right.

We have to remember to live our days to the fullest. We must thank God because every minute is a blessing. This is an important lesson. Never forget that the people who make a difference in our lives are not the ones with the most credentials, the most money, or the most awards. They are the ones who care for us. We must do our best to be kind because everyone you meet is fighting some kind of battle!

This story reminds me of the love our two-year-old daughter had for our month-old son. He was sleeping in the bassinet, and I was busy and hadn't noticed what was going on.

He started crying and screaming like something was wrong. When I looked into the bassinet, our daughter had blanketed our son with her toys. Some were a bit heavy for a newborn baby, but she just wanted to share her love for her toys with him.

Needed by My Sister

MY SISTER WAS LIVING in an assisted-living community on Merritt Island. Her husband passed away about a year ago. She is now living in Texas.

I go down to Merritt Island quite often to play bunco and celebrate birthdays with some of my close friends. If I could, I visit my sister for a while before I had to head back to Jacksonville. I like to get back before dark. It takes me about two hours.

The last time I went down, I had time to stop by and see her. When she came to the door, she didn't even say hello. She said, "Oh, you are just the person I need." My ears perked up because we all like to be needed. When we get to a certain age, we may get the idea that we are not of much worth anymore and not always needed. I quickly asked, "What do you need?" I hoped I would be able to meet her need.

When I got inside I saw all these things on the carpet: material, scissors, stapler, measuring tape, yardstick, and some other items she thought she might need for a project. She explained that she had purchased a footstool from an estate sale in the assisted-living location. She wanted to cover it, but the material she had purchased was too stiff. She couldn't get it to work. I sat down and started looking the situation over to see what could be done. I was hoping and praying I could meet this need.

She was trying to work on the floor, and for a couple of older ladies, working on the floor just didn't work. I suggested that we move some of the things on the small table and try working on it. She had no large table in her small apartment.

That seemed to work much better for our backs. I started working with the material and cut it to the size we needed. After folding it in the places it needed to be folded, we were able to start stapling. Her stapler used every muscle I had. I realized a few days later why my back and arms were aching. There was no way she could have ever done the stapling on her own. I am seven years younger, and it was very difficult for me.

I told her that I needed to leave by four because I liked to get home before dark. When we finally finished the project, it was four o'clock.

She was very thankful for my help and my strong muscles. A few days later, I found aching muscles that I didn't know I had. They hadn't been used for any work like that.

When I got ready to leave, someone knocked on her door. The lady asked, "Is your sister ready to go down?"

I asked, "Ready to go down for what?"

She said, "To go down to eat dinner."

I said, "Oh my gosh. What time is it?"

She informed me it was five o'clock—and not four. It quickly came to me that the time change had just happened, and she had not changed her clock. We laughed about it, and I still arrived home before dark. I was pleased that I could help my sister, and it was worth a few sore muscles. She is enjoying her little footstool and is very appreciative of my help. It helped my ego to know that I was still needed by someone.

My Woodworker

BACK IN THE SIXTIES, during one of our vacations, we found a furniture company called Habershams. They made very attractive furniture out of pine. I fell in love with it, and we decided to purchase several pieces for our country bedroom. I loved the four-poster bed, but it was very expensive. We both thought it would look great with the other pieces, but it was a little beyond our budget.

My husband inspected it all over and said, "I think I could make that."

I quickly said, "Really? Go for it." We took a picture and were able to get some literature from Habersham with pictures of the bed. When we arrived home, he couldn't wait to get started on it, which made me very happy. He is not one to put things off. If I need something done, he seems to enjoy pleasing me and marking it off the list.

He built it, and it was his very first woodworking project. It is beautiful and even has carving on. After forty years, we are still sleeping in that bed.

A few years later, he built me the most beautiful armoire to match the other Habersham furniture in our bedroom. It has shelves, drawers, and an inside place for our TV. It also has carvings of all kinds on the doors. It is my favorite of all the things he has made.

When we travel, we always look for nice furniture stores and take pictures of interesting or different things we find. I pick, and he builds. It's a great combination.

His love for woodworking really gives him a mental outlet from the office. His work at the office was procuring and completing projects for the space program, which was very stressful.

He finally retired from being an electrical and general contractor. It took five times before he finally decided to call it quits. He stays busy as a woodworker for friends, neighbors, and family. He also does electrical work and almost anything that people need help with. He is not one to sit around. This is great for him since he loves helping people.

Retirement Is Not Healthy for Some Men

I WAS CHECKING OUT AT the grocery store, and I started talking to the lady in front of me. We somehow got on the subject of our husbands' retirements. I said my husband had retired, but the company kept calling him back for certain jobs because of his credentials. He had retired five times.

She informed me that her husband had retired, but he went back to work because she thought he was going to die.

I quickly asked, "Why? What was the problem?"

She said, "Because I was going to kill him!"

What Would You Do?

AN ELDERLY MAN WAS heavily sedated. A bad stroke had left him pretty helpless.

A young man showed up to visit the elderly man.

The nurse said, "Sir, your son is here." She had to repeat it several times before he finally opened his eyes.

He could barely see the young pilot as he stood close to his bed. He couldn't move much of his body due to the stroke. He was able to move his right arm and reached out to the young man.

The pilot wrapped his strong hands around the old man's frail ones. He squeezed to let the old man know that he was sending a message of love and encouragement.

The nurse told him his father was very weak, and she didn't think he would make it through the night.

The light was very dim, and the pilot continued to hold the old man's hand through the night. He shared gentle words of love and strength.

The nurse tried to get the young man to take a rest for a while, but he continued by his bedside.

Sadly, the next morning, the old man went to be with the Lord.

The pilot finally let go of the man's lifeless hand and went to find the nurse.

While she did what she was expected to do, he just stood outside and waited.

When she finally returned, she said how sorry she was.

The pilot stopped her and asked, "Who was this man?"

The nurse looked at him with a very startled look. "What do you mean? He is your father."

"No, he wasn't," the pilot replied. "I never saw him before in my life."

"Then why didn't you say something when I took you to him?" she replied.

"I knew it was a mistake, but when you said he was expecting his son, and he wasn't there, I realized he was so sick that he wouldn't know whether I was his son or not. I just felt he needed me, so I stayed. I came here tonight to find Mr. Harry White. His son was killed in Iraq today, and I was sent to inform him. What was this gentleman's name?"

With tears in her eyes, the nurse said, "Mr. Harry White!"

The next time someone needs you, will you stay?

MoRe Laughs

CANDY WAS VISITING HER blonde best friend. Jeannie had just purchased two new dogs. Candy asked Jeannie what their names were.

Jeannie said that one was Rolex, and the other was Timex.

Candy said, "Whoever heard of someone naming their dogs like that?"

"Hello?" Jeannie said. "They're *watchdogs!*"

GeogRaphy

TWO BLONDES, GINGER AND Jane, lived in Tennessee. They were talking on a bench, and one blonde said, "Which do you think is farther away: Florida or the moon?"

The other blonde turned and said, "Hello, can you see Florida?"

DisNeyLaNd

TWO BLONDES, SUSY AND Cindy, were taking a trip to Disney. On the interstate, they saw a sign: "Disney LEFT." They started crying, turned around, and went home.

CRaP

A BLONDE, BRIDGETT, PUSHED HER BMW into a gas station and told the mechanic it died.

After he worked on it for a few minutes, it was idling smoothly. Bridgett said, "What's the problem?"

He replied, "Just crap in the carburetor."

She said, "How often do I have to do that?"

Duh!

Directions

A BLONDE, KELLY, WAS OUT for a walk. At the river, she saw another blonde on the opposite bank. "Yoo-hoo!" she shouted. "How can I get to the other side?"

The second blonde looked up the river and then down the river. She shouted, "You *are* on the other side."

Picture Lesson

MISS MARY WAS TRYING to help her students understand how blood flows in our bodies. She tried to give them a more visual picture of how it works.

She said, "If I stood on my head, where would the blood run?"

The children answered, "Into your head."

She replied, "Great. That's right, but how about when I'm standing upright—as we usually are? Why doesn't the blood run into our feet?"

A little guy in the back of the room shouted, "'Cause your feet aren't empty."

Who Won?

A COUPLE WAS DRIVING DOWN a country road for several miles, not saying a word. Earlier, a discussion had led to an argument—and neither of them wanted to concede their position.

As they passed a barnyard of mules, goats, and pigs, the husband asked sarcastically, "Relatives of yours?"

"Yep," the wife replied. "In-laws!"

Ouch!

Words

BILL READ AN ARTICLE to his wife about how many words women use a day—thirty thousand—to a man's fifteen thousand.

Sarah replied, "The reason is because women have to repeat everything to you men."

The husband turned to his wife and said, "What?"

Children Don't Miss Anything

THE CHILDREN AT THE Christian elementary school were lined up in the cafeteria for lunch. There was a large bowl of beautiful red apples. The teacher wrote on a piece of paper: "Take only one. God is watching."

As they moved down the line, there was a large plate full of chocolate chip cookies at the other end. A child had written a note: "Take all you want. God is watching the apples."

Kids Are Quick

IN SUNDAY SCHOOL, THE teacher was talking to her first graders about the importance of the Ten Commandments.

She said, "Is there a commandment that teaches us how to treat our brothers and sisters?"

Without hesitation, a little boy with younger siblings answered, "Thou shall not kill!"

My Husband's Trip to the Store

My HUSBAND IS RETIRED, but his hobby is woodworking. He builds all kinds of cabinetry, shelving, and beautiful furniture. He dresses pretty shabbily when he is working in the garage.

I happened to be out of town, and he had to take care of his own meals. He needed some ham for sandwiches and went down the street to the grocery store. They didn't have the ham we usually get, and he decided to go to the grocery store across the street.

On his way out of the store, he happened to see a table in front with some small spiral hams on it. The sign said: "One Dollar Off."

The hams were not what we usually got, but the price appealed to him. He picked one up and took it to the clerk at the counter.

She rang it up and said, "That will be ten dollars."

He said, "What about the sale? It says it's a dollar off."

She didn't know about that and called over the manager.

He checked it and said that it was off the original price.

My husband thought about it and decided he would go to the grocery across the street to get the ham that he knew he was supposed to get in the first place.

The clerk asked, "Do you want it?"

My husband said, "No, I don't want it."

He was thinking he would just get a ham at the other store that he knew I wanted.

He left the store in his shabby clothing and got into his truck. His window was down, and he heard someone yelling at him. A fellow in his twenties handed him the ham through the window.

My husband said, "That's not mine. I didn't pay for it."

The young man said, "I know, but I did." He immediately took off.

My husband yelled, "Thank you." He thought about what had happened. The thought came to him that someday he will stand before God—and God will have a list of things he had done. My husband will say to God, "I did not pay for that."

Jesus will say, "I know, but I did."

The Crash

Just OUTSIDE OUR BEDROOM door we have an étagère in our living room. It has five glass shelves that display many of the beautiful keepsakes we have purchased over the years. Many of them have been gifts. We purchased Hummel figurines in Germany when my husband was stationed there, beautiful pitchers, bowls, expensive bells, figurines, a bust of Moses with the Ten Commandments, a crystal cross, and another piece of glassware with Christ's handprint on it. These things mean a lot to both of us. Many memories are behind each piece.

Last week my husband got up at two o'clock in the morning as most men do after a certain age. He had recently hurt his back and thought he was going to take one of his pills.

I heard the étagère jingle, and the next sound was a horrible crash. I heard broken glass flying in a million pieces. I jumped out of bed, shouted my husband's name, and asked if he was all right. I was praying he wasn't underneath that mess.

He finally said, "I'm okay." He explained that he had been sleepwalking. When he opened the bedroom door to go out into the living room, he thought he was going outside to the truck. He thought he was opening the door of the truck. Unfortunately, when he pulled the truck door, it was really the leg of the étagère.

What a mess. All I could see was body parts of my Hummels—heads, arms, legs—and many other pieces of glass on the hardwood floor. Five large gold candleholders and candles were mixed in the mess.

I said, "We have to get our shoes on before we tackle this mess."

Because of his bad back, I insisted that I would pick up all the pieces that looked like they might have a chance of being saved and glued back together. I asked him to get the broom, vacuum, and a clean wastebasket to sweep up the small pieces.

The couch was across from the étagère and was leaning up, which helped. Many of the items had fallen onto the couch. The étagère and its five glass shelves were unharmed.

We cleaned up the worst and decided it was best to get some sleep and finish the mess in the morning. It was not something that we looked forward to waking up to, but we needed our sleep in order to have the energy to tackle it the next day.

The next day, it took us several hours to clean up all the glass. It seemed to have found every niche and corner of the living room. I didn't know glass could fly so far. The couch had to be vacuumed from top to bottom. We found pieces under the cushions too. It took me all day to get everything back in order. The étagère looked pretty bare, but I will thank God for saving some of my favorite large pieces. The bust of Moses, the crystal cross, the glass bookend with the imprint of Christ's hand, a painted pitcher, and the five gold candleholders were only missing a few chips. The five candles also made it through the catastrophe.

A few days later, my husband got up early. When I came into the kitchen, he said, "Honey, come over here." He was sitting at the desk where all the broken pieces had been. There, lined up as big as you please, all my Hummels were looking normal. He had the bells with the figurines that acted as handles partially glued and said he thought he could fix all of them.

In the next few days, he was glued to the desk, finishing what he had started on all the pieces. He even took the time to go through the wastebasket and the vacuum to find some of the pieces. In the next few days, it was like a miracle had been performed before our very eyes. Most of my keepsakes were back on the étagère. It was like they had never moved.

I know God values the things we value and think are important and have meaning in our lives. How many men would sit there for hours, putting all those back together again? My wonderful husband also loves and cares about what is important to me.

I said, "Honey, did you notice that I didn't get upset with you for doing this?"

He said, "Yes. That was the second miracle."

Quick Thinking

THE GAME WARDEN SAW this young guy, Carl, a real redneck, fishing and decided he needed to stop and talk to him. He noticed he had a chest sitting close by. "What you got in that chest, young man?"

"Oh, sir, I have my pet catfish in this here chest."

"Do you have a license to catch those catfish?"

"Oh, naw, sir. These are just my pet catfish, so I don't need them there licenses."

"Explain what you mean by pet catfish?" the warden said.

"Yes, sir. Pet catfish. I take these here catfish down to the lake every few days or so, and you wouldn't believe how much they enjoy swimming around for a while. I then blow a whistle, and you wouldn't believe how fast they jump right back into that there chest and home we go."

The warden looked at Carl and said, "Listen, young man. That is a bunch of baloney."

Carl said, "Mr. Government Man, I'm tellin' ya it works."

"Okay," the warden said. "You have to show me."

Carl said, "Yes, sir. I will be glad to do just that." He quickly poured the catfish into the lake and stood back.

After several minutes, the warden said, "Well?"

Carl said "Well, what?"

The warden said. "When are you going to call them back? I don't have all day."

"Call what or who back?" Carl asked.

The warden said, "The pet catfish."

"Sir, what pet catfish?"

Who outsmarted who?

More than Milk

THE NINETY-NINE-YEAR-OLD MOTHER HAD been ill and was dying in her home in Scotland. Her loving and concerned family gathered around her and tried to console her. They were sure she was going home to see her Lord soon.

Warm milk is an old-fashioned remedy when someone is not feeling well. They offered it to her, but after tasting it, she shook her head.

A younger relative took the glass back to the kitchen and remembered a bottle of whiskey that had been given to them a year ago. She opened it and poured a good amount into the warm milk.

Rushing back to the old mother's bedside, they held the glass to her lips. She was weak, but she drank a little. She nodded her head for more, and before they knew it, she had finished the whole glass—down to the last drop. She perked up a bit and even seemed to be smiling.

One of the children said, "Mother, please, do you feel like sharing some of your wise words with us before leaving us?"

She raised herself up in bed, looked at them, and said, "Whatever you do, don't sell that cow."

We Need Fixed

A FRIEND SHARED THIS STORY with me, and it was just too good and so appropriate to where we are in life today. This is about a coach, and if I told you his name, some of you would recognize him from the story I am about to share.

Several of my friends and I were baseball coaches. We attended a conference years ago. While we were waiting in line, we heard other guys talking about who was going to be speaking. One name kept surfacing, and we overheard one coach saying, "Oh, man—worth every penny of my airfare."

We all looked at each other and had not heard of this person. We were all young coaches and hadn't come to know that much of the baseball world. We mainly came to the conference to have a good time together and maybe learn something.

When they brought the man out onstage and introduced him, everyone went crazy. We all perked up and said, "Wow, we better sit up and listen good." This man was quite old and had been retired for several years. He shuffled to the stage with his polyester pants, a light blue shirt, and a home plate hanging from a string around his neck. We again all looked at one another and wondered who the guy was.

After speaking for a while, he seemed to notice that some of us in the room seemed to be snickering. *Where is this guy going with this—or has he forgotten about the home plate hanging around his neck?*

Finally, he said, "You're probably all wondering why I'm wearing home plate around my neck."

The audience laughed.

He said, "I may be old, but I'm not crazy. The reason I stand before you today is to share with you baseball people what I've learned in my life … and what I've learned about home plate in my old age. Let me ask you a question: Do you know how wide home plate is in Little League?"

After a pause, someone said, "Seventeen inches?"

"That's right," he said. "How about in Babe Ruth's day. Any Babe Ruth coaches in the house?"

After another pause, someone reluctantly said, "Seventeen inches?"

"Right again. How many high school coaches do we have in the room?"

Hundreds of hands went up, and they began to catch on.

He asked, "How wide is home plate in high school baseball?"

"Seventeen inches," they answered in confidence.

"You're right!" Then he went to the college coaches and said, "How wide is home plate in college?"

"Seventeen inches!" they said in unison.

"Any minor league coaches here? How wide is home plate in pro ball?"

"Seventeen inches!"

"Right! And in the Major Leagues? How wide is home plate in the Major Leagues?"

"Seventeen inches!"

"Seventeen inches!" he confirmed, his voice now bellowing off the walls. "And what do they do with a big league pitcher who can't throw the ball over seventeen inches? What they don't do is this. They don't say, 'Ah, that's okay, Jimmy. If you can't hit a seventeen-inch target, we'll make it eighteen inches or nineteen inches. We'll make it twenty inches so you have a better chance of hitting it. If you can't hit that, let us know so we can make it wider still ... say twenty-five inches.' Coaches, what do we do when your best player shows up late to practice? Or when our team rules forbid facial hair and a guy shows up unshaven? What if he gets caught drinking? Do we hold him accountable? Do we change the rules to fit him? Do we widen home plate?"

The laughter and chuckles gradually faded as four thousand coaches grew quiet. The fog lifted as the old coach's message began to unfold. He turned the plate toward himself and drew something with a Sharpie. When he turned it toward the crowd, a house was revealed—complete with a door and two windows.

"This is the problem in our homes today. With our discipline. We don't teach accountability to our kids, and there is no consequence for failing to meet standards. We just widen the plate!"

At the top of the house, he added a small American flag. "This is the problem in our schools today. The quality of our education is going downhill fast, and teachers have been stripped of the tools they need to be successful and educate and discipline our young people. We are allowing others to widen home plate. Where is that getting us?"

There was silence.

He replaced the flag with a cross. "And this is the problem in the church. Powerful people in positions of authority have taken advantage of young children—only to have such atrocities swept under the rug for years. Our church leaders are widening home plate for themselves. And we allow it.

"And the same is true with our government. Our so-called representatives make rules for us that don't apply to themselves. They take bribes from lobbyists and foreign countries. They no longer serve us. And we allow them to widen home plate. We see our country falling into a dark abyss—and we just watch."

We were all amazed. At a baseball conference, I had expected to learn something about curveballs, bunting, and how to run better practices. I had learned something far more valuable from an old man with home plate strung around his neck. I had learned something about life, about myself, about my own weaknesses, and about my responsibilities as a leader. I had to hold myself and others accountable to that which I knew to be right, lest our families, our faith, and our society continue down an undesirable path.

The speaker said, "If I am lucky, you will remember one thing from this old coach today. If we fail to hold ourselves to a higher standard, a standard of what we know to be right, if we fail to hold our spouses and our children to the same standards, if we are unwilling or unable to provide a consequence when they do not meet the standard, and if our schools and churches and our government fail to hold themselves accountable to those they serve, there is but one thing to look forward to." He held home plate in front of his chest, turned it around, and revealed its black backside. "We have dark days ahead! Coaches, keep your players—no matter how good they are—your own children, your churches, your government, and, most of all, yourself at seventeen inches. And this, my friends, is what our country has become and what is wrong with it today. Go out there and fix it! Don't widen the plate."

Printed in the United States
By Bookmasters